ROADSCHOOLING

The Ultimate Guide to
Education Through Travel

Nancy Sathre-Vogel

www.roadschooling.com

ROADSCHOOLING
The Ultimate Guide to Education Through Travel

Published in the United States by:

Old Stone Publishing

ISBN 978-0-9837187-4-1

Table of Contents

Introduction

> **Will my kids learn everything they need to know?**
>
> **Will I be able to keep up with my children's education on the road?**
>
> **Will I harm my children so they'll never be able to live a normal life?**

These are questions most parents ask before setting out to travel long term. Will the travel be good for my kids? Will they keep with their peers?

The answers to all of those questions are both yes and no. Your children will never learn everything they need to know, you'll do just fine educating them, you won't harm them, and yes the travel will be good for them.

I get a fair number of emails from people around the world asking me how to roadschool their children. They're wanting to take off and travel for a year or more and are wondering how to fit schooling in with travel. How, exactly, does that marriage work?

Travel is one of the best educations you can give your children. Not only will they learn all the basic 'school stuff,' but they'll learn a lot more as well.

In this book, I will cover all the basics of taking advantage of your travels to educate your children. We'll start with the basics, and then talk specifics. If you take only one thing away from this book, please walk away with the idea that you CAN do it and your children will be better for it.

Who am I and why am I writing this book? I am a teacher with 21 years of classroom experience and hold a BA Ed. in Special Education and MA Ed. in Integrated Math & Science. My master's thesis was on brain research as it applies to learning. My husband also happens to be a long-term teacher as well, with an MA Ed. in Technology in Education.

In addition to that practical and theoretical basis, I road-schooled my twin sons for four years. We spent their third grade year cycling around the USA and Mexico, and we took advantage of that year to help our sons learn about American history. Their fifth, sixth, and seventh grades were spent cycling from Alaska to Argentina, where we learned a very wide variety of topics. The whole time, we took advantage of our travels as the basis of their education. The only curriculum materials we carried were for math.

You are probably asking how they did; how they compare to their peers. After four years of a very atypical education, did they 'keep up' with other kids who went through a more traditional approach to education? The answer is yes, and then some.

I'll tell you up front that one of my sons is very highly gifted. Traditional academics were never a concern for him, as any kind of academic pursuit comes easily. He was advanced before we started traveling, and continues to be advanced now. Our other son, however, is a fairly normal, average type of kid. I think his performance is more along the lines of what one could reasonably expect from a roadschooling lifestyle. He was on level, or slightly below, in most academics before we headed out. Now he is significantly ahead. I will explain more throughout this book.

How do I do it?

One day, I got this email from Merlijn from the UK asking me some excellent questions that many parents have. She addresses questions that leave many parents perplexed.

> *Dear Nancy,*
> *Road schooling is my major concern and I am wondering if you can help put my mind to ease. How have you managed to keep up the education of your boys while on the road? How did you actually integrate education in your travels.*
> *I realize that learning opportunities are all around us, but at the moment I find it difficult to imagine how we can do it while bike touring and actually do some miles. Do you stop at every opportunity (which would mean a lot of stops, but not a*

lot of mileage)? Do you look up certain sites of interest (historic, architectural, natural) and make a project of it? Did you take a certain time per day to work on subjects or did you discuss things on the bike?

Taking advantage of where you are and the sites around you is a great way to inspire your children to consider things they never would have thought about.

This is truly a complicated question with many different aspects to address. In this book, I'll do my best to explain our approach and how we dealt with it during our four years of travel on bicycle, and will also present many case studies of other long-term traveling families. Be aware that there are as many different ways of roadschooling as there are families wanting to do it.

What is Education?

> *Education is not the filling of a bucket, but the lighting of a fire.*
>
> William Butler Yeats

It's funny how we associate the words education and learning with school. In many parents' minds, a brick building broken into classrooms and filled with desks and chairs and blackboards means learning. School = education = learning. Synonyms all three.

And yet, are they? What is education? What is true learning?

Kids are naturally curious and have an innate desire to make sense of the world around them. In other words – they want to learn. Have you ever seen your child out digging in the ground, trying to pull earthworms out of the dirt? And then that same child proudly shows you all the segments and explains how the worm wiggles to move? She is simply trying to put the pieces together to make sense of what's around her.

Kids have an inborn inclination to want to make sense of their world. Education is the process of learning that.

Seeing wildlife in their natural habitat will spark an interest in ways that books simply cannot.

I've been asked repeatedly about 'holes' in my sons' education. Would they know everything they were 'supposed' to know? How were we ensuring their education was up to 'standards?'

My question in return was: What are the standards? How are they defined? And then I could answer my own question: They are pretty much random.

As a 21-year veteran of classroom teaching, I served on my share of curriculum committees. I sat there for hour after hour hammering out a curriculum; a list of standards that kids would learn. I also saw just how random that list was. If I learned one thing from my adventures in and out of the classroom, it was that schools don't have all the answers.

Don't get me wrong – the idea behind a curriculum is fine. They try to ensure that each child learns the same things as another, regardless of which teacher he/she has. I suppose there is value in knowing that all children entering fourth grade in a particular school will know the phases of the moon or the parts of a flower. It makes it easier for the fourth grade teacher if all her students have the same base.

But really, does it matter if a kid learns about the phases of the moon in third grade or seventh? Is there something magic about being ten years old that makes it easier/more effective/more real/more whatever to learn about the history of your state at that age? Does it really matter when a kid learns something? And is a particular state's history really one of those must-knows?

My perspective is that it doesn't really matter *what* a child learns, just *that* he learns. Understanding how to go about learning something will go a lot further than memorizing a particular set of dates or figures. As long as your child is learning – and learning how to learn – it's all good.

How Kids Learn

Kids learn. They just learn. Their brains are designed to make sense of the world around them and if they are placed in a challenging, stimulating environment, they will learn.

One of my favorite stories to illustrate how easy it is to educate kids on the road is the one about my son Davy learning to read. Daryl had always been a strong reader – he started reading at age 4 and loved to read to his brother. Davy loved the books and the two of them shared many, many hours engrossed in books – Daryl reading and Davy listening. I'm sure because of that, Davy never felt a need to learn to read on his own.

In grade 1, Davy tested well below grade level in reading. We spent many evenings having him read to us, and by 2nd grade he was at grade level – barely. He struggled to keep up with the rest of the class and was a pretty reluctant reader.

In 3rd grade, we took our twins out of school and started biking. For the first few months, we were pretty overwhelmed by the logistics of biking all day and planning a route and finding food and water. Needless to say, we didn't read with the kid at all. Every night we curled up in the tent and read a bedtime story to the boys, but Davy didn't read a single word – or so we thought.

Reading is the best way to learn to read. Encourage your children to read anything and everything.

Then one day it was pouring rain and we made the decision to stay put – riding in cold rain is no fun! So there we were, four of us crammed into a tiny tent ALL DAY as rain poured from the heavens. What to do?

Our bedtime story at the time was Where the Red Fern Grows (about a 4th grade level) so I read and read and read until I couldn't read any more. Then I handed the book to my husband and he read and read and read. Then I read some more. Then

John. We handed the book to Daryl and he read. We started taking turns – I read a chapter, then John, then Daryl. We skipped Davy because he couldn't read (or so we thought).

I'm still not sure why, but finally John handed the book to Davy and asked him to read a chapter. I was mortified. It was one of those situations where your stomach does a flip flop and you know your kid is about to be humiliated but you're powerless to do anything about it.

The kid surprised me – he read it flawlessly! I'm serious – completely, totally fluently. At a fourth grade level and he was just a few months into third grade!

That experience taught me that kids learn. In spite of their teachers. In spite of all our fancy-schmancy, new-fangled, electronic gadgets designed to teach. Kids' brains are designed to learn – that's what they do.

We learn when our brains create dendrites – physical connections between brain cells. Each person walking this earth was born with all the brain cells they will ever have – somewhere around 100 billion of them. That's a 1 with eleven zeros behind it. In other words, that's a lot of brain cells. Those cells, however, are pretty much worthless unless they are connected together, and that's the job of dendrites.

Dendrites are physical connections within the brain that join cells together. Each brain cell (neuron) can be connected with up to 15,000 other neurons, creating a complex network for messages to whiz from one part of the brain to another.

The more dendrites we have, the more 'connected' the neurons, the easier it is to learn anything – it's easier to find a 'hook' to something else you already know so therefore it's easier to fit the new knowledge in and have it make sense. Growing dendrites only happens when you are in a challenging, stimulating environment.

Think about learning a new video game. At first it's a challenge – you have to reason through everything and try to make sense of it and figure out how all the pieces fit together, but once you've mastered it, it's easy. At that point you can do it on autopilot. That's because it was hard growing those dendrites in the first place, but once they are in place, they are there.

As we travel, our kids are always in new and stimulating environments, therefore their brains are always growing dendrites which makes it easier for them to learn anything. It appears as though their brains are so stimulated by everything that is going on around them that they just pick stuff up – it seems to go in through osmosis.

Does this mean kids must travel in order to learn efficiently? Absolutely not. As long as they are in a stimulating environment that challenges them to think and reason and explore new things, they are growing. It's just that it's easier to get kids in those challenging and stimulating environments while traveling.

What is Roadschooling?

Education doesn't have to take place within the confines of four walls, and roadschoolers have learned to take full advantage of that fact. Many families have opted out of a 'traditional' education, and have chosen instead to take their children out to see the world – whether in RVs, planes, buses, or bicycles. Roadschooling families make a conscious effort to capitalize on children's natural penchant toward learning. They go out of their way to visit historical and/or scientific sites in order to arouse that sense of curiosity in children.

As families travel throughout the world visiting historical sites, children gain an understanding of the world around them. They'll understand what life was like on the fields of Gettysburg or in ancient Mayan cities by being there. They visit museums and national parks and natural wonders. Roadschooling parents encourage their children to learn from everything surrounding them and the kids learn in a natural learning environment.

Learning takes place around the clock, wherever you happen to be. Education is a lifestyle, with the whole family taking advantage of a visit to a battlefield to learn about the Civil War or learning how locks work during a visit to the Panama Canal.

Remember there is no one right way. Each child, each parent, and each family is different and has unique wants, needs, desires, skills.

Learning happens everywhere. Education is not limited to a few hours a day or to certain places.

My personal philosophy on parenting is that I want to give my children options. As many as possible. For that reason, I feel it's imperative that I prepare my children for university. Others feel that is not necessary at all. Ultimately, it is up to each parent to decide which direction to take to educate your children. For all of us, however, taking advantage of travel experiences is a great way to go.

Roadschooling Reading

Children are made readers on the laps of their parents.

Emilie Buchwald

Reading. It's essential. It's basic to our ability to navigate our world. If our kids aren't reading, then we, as parents, worry.

Way back in 1995 when I was about to teach first grade for the very first time, I was terrified. I knew how to teach kids to read better, but had no clue how to teach them to read in the first place. A friend of mine gave me the best advice ever: "Don't worry," he said. "The kids will learn to read in spite of what you do."

And that's true. All kids need in order to learn how to read is the desire and opportunity to do so. Create the desire by reading yourself. Read to your children, read with your children, have books around, encourage them to read whatever they see. That's all it takes. They'll read.

As they develop into stronger readers, continue to encourage reading by choosing environments rich with words. Take time to actually read the explanations on displays at museums, have books in the car, read everything you can. It works, it really does.

As traveling, roadschooling parents, it's hard to know how much time to dedicate to reading instruction. Do we take time out of our experiences in the real world to sit down with workbooks to help our children learn? Or do we carry on, hoping they'll somehow figure it out?

I think it's important to understand the process of reading in order to know what to focus on.

When it comes to the instruction of reading, the deepest, most profound impact on my instructional thoughts and ideas came from reading The Read Aloud Handbook by Jim Trelease. That book, single-handedly, changed how I taught reading in my classroom and how I've worked with my own children. I encourage every parent to buy the book and read it.

The basic idea behind read aloud is that language development comes in a hierarchy, and if we're consciously aware of that process, we can foster its growth.

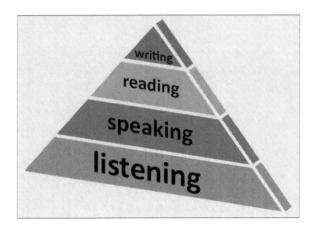

The base of all language arts skills is listening comprehension. We start working on that from the day our children are born by talking to them. We read them books that use different vocabulary from what we use in our day-to-day life. As children hear us speak and read books, they hear various words and figure out their meaning from the context of how they are used.

Sadly, some parents don't read to their children at all, or they stop doing so at an early age. That is the single most damaging thing a parent can do to prevent their children from learning to read and enjoy it. On the flip side, parents who do read to their children daily are doing the best possible activity to promote reading.

Researchers have found that listening is the base for everything else.

If kids hear words being used, then they will eventually be able to use those words in their own spoken language, and then they'll be able to read them and write them. None of the other categories will move upward if that listening part stagnates.

That's where the whole read aloud thing comes into play.

When parents read to their children, they read more advanced books than the children would be capable of reading on their own. Generally speaking, a child's listening comprehension is at least two years ahead of his reading capability. Children will naturally ask for books at their comprehension level and, through listening to books at a higher level than they could read, you are introducing more advanced vocabulary.

Once children orally comprehend the advanced vocabulary, you'll see that transfer to their speaking, reading and, finally, their writing.

Read to your child. Read aloud will promote an interest in stories and provide the background and vocabulary basis to build upon.

It should come as no surprise that reading to kids is not travel-exclusive. No matter where you live or what you are doing, reading to your children will provide the basis for their further education.

We made a bedtime story a nightly routine and always made time for a story before going to sleep. No matter where we were – in our tent, a hotel, or the house of strangers – we read to our children before going to sleep.

Make bedtime stories a habit. You'll be doing your child a huge favor.

And then what, you ask? In addition to reading *to* your child, read *with* your child. Get some basic children's books and read them together. You will read them the first time or two (or five), while following along with your finger. Eventually, your child will be able to 'read' part of the story – it's really memorized, but they think they're reading. Do the same with nursery rhymes.

Once your child is comfortable with 'reading,' ask him to point to certain words in the story. For example, if you're reading twinkle, twinkle little star, you could ask your child to point to the word star. He will go through the writing, saying each word as he points to it until he finds star. Congratulate him, then ask him to point to the word twinkle.

All of this can be done in the normal course of the day. You don't need to consciously set aside time for 'reading.' Whenever you find you have a few minutes, put your child on your lap and pick up a book. You will be amazed at how quickly he learns to read.

> *Reading aloud with children is known to be the single most important activity for building the knowledge and skills they will eventually require for learning to read.*
>
> Marilyn Jager Adams

Start reading to your children from an early age so they develop a love of story.

Roadschooling Writing and Researching

This is probably the easiest area to take advantage of your travels – you'll have lots of interesting topics to research and write about!

There are two distinct skills you'll want to work on: free writing, and the whole writing process. Free writing is the idea of simply getting words on paper. Spelling, punctuation, and grammar don't matter. Think of this as when you write yourself a note – as long as you can understand it, it's all good.

The writing process means going through the whole process to create a polished document. You'll edit and revise, and revise and edit, and then edit some more until the writing is perfect.

For free writing skills, have your child keep a journal of his experiences. These writings should be completely unedited. You simply want your child to get in the habit of writing down his thoughts. It doesn't matter what he writes about; it's the process of writing that counts.

For some children, keeping a very nice journal/scrapbook is very motivating. Your child can write daily entries, but also put in entrance tickets, photos, postcards, or other odds and ends from the day. Having colored pencils and glue on hand will encourage him to do a nice job on his journal.

Certain experiences, like visiting the Panama Canal, are catalysts for in-depth research and writing. Choose your topics well to make sure there is enough information available in order to reduce frustration.

Every week or month (depending on how much you feel you need to work with him), have your child pick one of his journal entries to edit. You can work with him on spelling, grammar, punctuation, etc. With help, your child should be able to produce a perfectly edited journal entry. As you work on these, you will start to see improvements in his free writing as well.

Of course, kids need to learn more than just journal writing. They also need to learn paragraph development, five-paragraph essays, and more. We worked on those skills separately from journaling.

For those more advanced skills, we tied our sons' writing with researching during our travels. Our kids researched what we were seeing and wrote essays about them. That gave us a chance to work with the boys on figuring out the research skills and also to help them edit their writing to perfection. Research took the form of both internet research and interviews with various people.

There are a number of different strategies you can use for these essays. Our favorite, and the one we used when we were organized and planning ahead, was to research the site in advance so we had an idea of what we would see. That helped advance our learning at the site tremendously, and allowed us to delve in more deeply.

An example of the planning ahead method was when we were arriving at the Panama Canal. We knew in advance that we would be there, and we had plenty of time as we waited for Davy's toe surgery to heal before we could move on. We took advantage of that time to research many different aspects of the Panama Canal – the ecological impact of connecting the oceans, the engineering challenges of building the canal, the physics involved in raising and lowering ships, and the mechanics of opening and closing the gates that held back the water.

When we arrived at the canal, our children already had a good idea what they would see and seeing it in action cemented what they had read about. In addition, new questions arose and they spent quite some time talking with the docents in the canal museum.

After the visit, our sons then wrote essays about some aspect of the canal. While writing the essays, I had a chance to work with them on the planning and outlining for the essay, as well as the actual writing and editing.

As you might imagine, we weren't always that organized, and we didn't always know what was coming up. There were many times when we stumbled upon an historical site, so we went in and learned what we could learn. We found our learning was more shallow in these circumstances, but we accepted that as a normal part of travel. After these surprise discoveries, we frequently asked our sons to write what we called 'quickies' – write everything they could think of about the site in five minutes. These quickies were a great exercise for the children in that they needed to just write, not think.

The most important thing to think about in terms of writing is that kids need to write in order to learn to write. Encourage them to write every chance you can.

History of the Panama Canal
By Davy

The Panama Canal is a connection between the Pacific and Atlantic Oceans. Ships can cut through the canal rather than going all the way around South America. The Panama Canal took 33 years to make, from 1881 to 1914. It is 51 miles long.

The French started building the Panama Canal. They were trying to make a flat river between the Pacific and the Atlantic oceans. At that time there were no bulldozers or dump trucks. They cut through the lowest and narrowest part between the two oceans. The French were trying to do it all by hand. That didn't work very well. First of all, they were trying to dig a steep walled canyon and the rock wasn't as strong as they had thought. There were lots of landslides. Secondly, they were moving huge boulders with nothing but muscle. Lots of men were leaving because they just couldn't take all the work. And thirdly, many of the men that stayed fell sick due to poor housing conditions and couldn't work. The French left in 1899.

In 1904, the Americans started working on the remains of the French work. They decided to use something called locks in order to raise the boats up and over the hill between the two oceans. There are many types of locks. The type they used worked by getting water into a no-ceiling room, raising the ship up. They did not use pumps; instead they use gravity.

Each lock has two artificial lakes. If a ship comes in on the bottom, they open the first set of doors, then they open the gate of the top lake and water rushes in to raise the ship. They make the water in the lock even with the water level in the next segment of the canal. Then the doors higher up open to allow the ship to pass into the canal. No water rushes out because the water is even with the new water level. The ship can just come out. It is the same with top to bottom except they empty the water into the bottom lake. A lock can raise or lower a ship 17 feet. Over all you need to go up about 85 feet to get through the Panama Canal.

Since both the oceans are about the same level, why raise and lower the ships? Because they would go over the mountains rather than go through them. There are a lot of reasons for that, but the main ones are for ecological reasons – they don't want to mix the water from the two oceans, and because it was easier to build locks than to dig out all the dirt and rock between the oceans.

The ships are pulled through the Panama Canal by engines called mules. Usually there are six mules per ship. About 12,500 ships come through each year. A private sailboat costs about $2,000 to cross. The cost depends on how big and how heavy it is. Once, a swimmer swam across it for thirty six cents. I don't think you are allowed to swim through it now. I think that the swimmer was doing a long distance swim or something that the government allowed.

Roadschooling Mathematics

Mathematics, in our opinion, was the one area we were not able to adequately use our journey for. For younger kids (approximately under the age of 8 or so) everything they need in terms of mathematics can quite easily be worked in to your travels, but once they get into higher math, not so.

All younger kids need is an understanding of the number system and how to manipulate numbers with addition, subtraction, multiplication, and division. All of these are easily incorporated into your travels. Have your child total up the amounts you spend in restaurants or stores, calculate gas mileage for your vehicle, figure out how many miles are left to the destination, etc...

Once a child reaches a level of needing to manipulate fractions, decimals, and algebraic equations, it will be much harder to build a complete program into your travels. There will be many times when you can bring in real-life examples based on your experiences, but not the entire program.

For that level, we carried math books with us on the bikes and our sons worked through them in hotels or campgrounds.

One of the most common questions I get is about the pacing – did we set aside time every day for the kids to work on math? The answer is no.

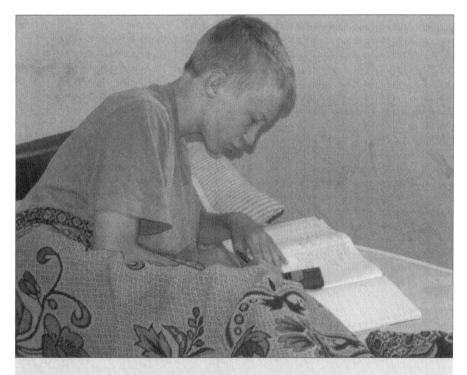

Our sons worked through math books at their own pace. We worked on math on our down days, rather than forcing the issue when we were busy with other activities.

On very busy days when we had a lot going on, their math books stayed packed away. On rest days, the boys worked on math. Some days they did one lesson; other days they did three or four lessons. It all depended on what was going on around us, how much time we had, and how tired we were.

Roadschooling Social Studies

One of the things I learned from my many years of teaching and serving on curriculum committees is that schools don't have all the answers. There is no magic set of knowledge that all kids need to learn.

Is it imperative that Americans learn about the Civil and Revolutionary Wars and Argentinians learn about the Falkland War? That's up to individual parents: if you feel it's important that your child know the history of your own country, then make sure you visit historical sites or build that history into your life.

The beauty of roadschooling is that you've got a delightful 'curriculum' at your fingertips. You are visiting historical sites that will bring history to life. You'll be meeting people of all walks of life. You are living 'social studies.' I've got a whole list of ways to extend that learning later in this book, but for now, let's walk through a particular experience in my own children's lives.

Take advantage of local history! Our stop in the staging ground for the Argentine military during the Falklands War sparked a big lesson into the causes of wars in general.

One of the questions we grappled with was this: does it really matter if kids learn about the Civil War or Falklands War or Vietnam War? Do the specifics matter or is the important thing the overarching themes behind the reasons behind the wars? If children learn about one or two wars in depth, does that information transfer to other wars?

My experience has shown me that what's important is that kids understand there are two sides to any war. The winner is not necessarily 'right' or 'better' than the loser. Once kids understand that idea, they are capable of understanding all wars.

As we traveled, we landed in Puerto San Julian along the Atlantic coast of Argentina for a few days. The area was rich with history so we took advantage of our time there to learn about the history of our world. We visited a life-sized replica of Magellan's ship and learned about his voyage and how they wintered in San

Julian because the weather was too severe to travel. Okay, then – we could check that one off the curriculum. Yes, that is on the traditional school curriculum.

But San Julian also happened to be the staging ground for the Argentine military during the Falklands War in 1982. For the Argentine people, the war is recent and very meaningful. Emotions, even though thirty years have passed, are still raw and jagged. The pain of defeat is still evident. Extraordinarily evident.

To make the lesson come even more alive, we happened to be in San Julian with a British cycling friend so we heard the story from both points of view. In short, we were living history for a few days.

Some would argue that learning about the Falklands War is nothing more than useless trivia – after all, it's not in the curriculum. It's not 'supposed' to be taught.

I beg to differ.

My sons saw history up close and personal while we were staying in San Julian. They saw an actual warplane with pictures of the six British ships it sank painted on its side. They heard the stories from both sides. They heard about a ruthless, egomaniacal dictator and an obstinate, pigheaded prime minister. They saw the folly and the wisdom on both sides of the argument. They understand why Argentina invaded and why Britain fought back. Who's right? The jury is still out.

But the lessons here go so much deeper. Just as there were many, many reasons for the Falklands War, so were there many reasons for any other war in history. The American Revolutionary War was, in many regards, similar to the Falklands. The Civil War? Certainly some parallels. WWI? WWII? The Vietnam War?

Once the idea of the 'causes' of war became clear, it was only a short step to consider the causes of other wars. And they all come down to two sides; two stories. We talked about them all with our sons.

So I ask you – is there a 'hole' in my sons' comprehension of history? Or is a comprehensive understanding of the intricacies of world politics sufficient?

As you travel, seek out historical sites from all eras. Climb on 1000-year-old Mayan ruins when you travel Mexico. Play hide and seek on Civil War battlefields in Pennsylvania. Visit Native American reservations and national monuments dedicated to Native American struggles to learn about the early days of the United States. Keep your eyes and ears open, and you will find out about historical sites all over.

If I have one word of advice for teaching Social Studies it's this: take advantage of where you are. Don't get hung up on following a curriculum or some set list of ideas. What matters is that your child gains an understanding of the cultures, people, and history of the world. If he's getting that, then all is well.

Roadschooling Science

Science is probably the area that is hardest to teach because it's so vast. The amount of knowledge and information in our world is doubling and tripling at an astounding rate. In the past, it was conceivably possible to teach kids pretty much all the science they needed to know. Today, that's impossible.

Ultimately, the actual content kids learn doesn't matter. Given the vast amount of information out there, it doesn't matter if a child learns the phases of the moon, the parts of a flower, the nitty-gritty of how surface tension works, or the systems of the human body. What's important is that they learn the process of figuring all that stuff out, and that they know where to find the info.

If you compare roadschooling to the typical school curriculum (in the USA anyway), it's a pretty good comparison. One school might teach astronomy and carbon dating, while another teaches properties of matter and cell formation. One roadschooling family might spend time at the Grand Canyon studying the geological layers of the earth while another visits the Florida Everglades and studies ecosystems.

Science is all around us. Don't worry about trying to teach the specific topics that kids back home would be learning. Learning about starfish and tidal pools may not be in the science book, but it's just as valuable.

In the end, it doesn't matter what content your child learns. What matters is that he understands that there is an enormous amount of information out there and how to find out about it if he wants to.

As you travel, you will naturally fall into many situations that can be exploited for educational purposes. Climbing up a sand dune? Talk about the forces of nature that break rocks into smaller particles to create sand. Camping out? Talk about the weather patterns and how those happen.

In short, take advantage of where you are and what is happening around you.

One time we cycled past Twisted Mountain, a large rock outcropping with amazing twisted rock layers throughout. We took advantage of that moment to talk with our sons about both the deposition of those layers of rocks millions of years ago, and the pushing and shoving effects of tectonic plates that created the twisted effect.

After cycling through Central America where we dealt with heat and humidity day after day, we finally climbed up into the Andes. The morning we crossed the equator, Davy remarked about how cold it was – and that he had been taught in school about how hot it was – at the equator. That led to a wonderful discussion about the correlation between elevation and temperature.

National and state parks are fabulous resources in the area of science, as they are frequently built around places of scientific interest.

How much time needs to be spent on schooling?

"A school day is about five hours, and that doesn't even include homework time. How can I make sure my children will learn just as much (and hopefully more) while traveling? I like to believe education is not as efficient at school as it can be at home (or the road) since there's only one teacher with twenty or more children, and at school is less likely to be child-led. Nevertheless, it seems like you still need a lot of time per week where education is the main goal."

You'd be surprised. When your life revolves around education, you end up spending very little time on it.

I know that sounds weird. What I'm trying to say is that as you travel, you'll be doing this stuff anyway. You'll go to national parks and explore the visitor centers and listen to ranger talks. That's all 'school.' You'll take hikes around battlefields and talk about the wars that happened there as you walk. That's 'school' too.

When you are traveling, your whole life will revolve around learning. When you visit a glacier, you'll learn about glaciers. You'll learn about sand dunes when you climb them. Learning is a lifestyle.

Every time you visit a cheese factory or a zoo, when you play in tidal pools along the coast or race up sand dunes, it's 'school.' Take advantage of every opportunity to get out and play, and your kids will be in school all the time.

In the evenings, after a long day of playing tourist, you'll need some down time – that's when your kids will reach for books to relax with. There's your reading for the day. Before they go to bed, have them spend a few minutes writing a journal entry, then read their bedtime story.

You don't have to stress about it – you really don't.

I know some people want more structure in their lives than others. The idea of leaving things up to chance doesn't sit well with everybody. If you are one of those people, I would encourage you to set a loose schedule, but don't worry about it. If the schedule doesn't work out some days, so be it.

When we were on our bike trip, our children's 'school' varied tremendously. On busy days where we spent many hours on the road, we simply talked about Mother Nature's handiwork or the weather patterns or the type of clouds in the sky. On our days off, the boys did their math while my husband and I did the many hum-drum tasks that needed to be done. When I had time, we sat down and did some research together.

Allow your 'regular' schedule to dictate your 'homeschooling' schedule rather than the other way around. Fit your schoolwork in around what you want to do and trust that it'll be okay. Honest, it will.

Formalizing Education

All the varied experiences are great and all, but if kids don't have the language to communicate what they know from climbing jagged rocks and running around in canyons, that's a problem. I have absolutely no idea if there is an official term for this, but I call the next step the formalization process.

For example, my sons rode their bikes the length of the Baja peninsula. They had looked at the map and seen the long arm of land jutting out into the ocean. When they got to the southern end, they got on a ferry to the mainland because there was no land route across. They 'knew' what that peninsula was all about. They cycled all thousand miles of it.

Yet they never knew it was called a peninsula. If someone had asked them about peninsulas, they would have responded that they had no idea, even though they knew more about them than most people. We needed to take their education to that formalization stage and give them the word for what they already knew. It just takes a few seconds once they understand the idea behind the vocabulary, but it's a necessary step.

The trouble is that we don't even think about it. It's not a conscious thought that we need to teach that vocabulary to our children. We're living life, and vocabulary lessons aren't a part of it.

Don't dismiss local schools! We put our children in local schools in both Honduras and Peru for a couple weeks each. It was a great way to learn Spanish, and get to know some local kids.

A good guide you could use would be to have some science and social studies texts from school and jump around in the book to coincide with what you are doing. That way you have an idea of what kinds of words the kids will be expected to know. For example, when you visit the Grand Canyon, use the section in the book about geology to know what kinds of words kids are expected to know and help them learn the vocabulary.

While it's a good idea to help your kids learn the vocab, I wouldn't worry much about it. We pulled our kids out of school for third grade to cycle around the USA and Mexico. They went back to fourth grade and came home complaining that they were lost – the other kids had learned a whole lot of stuff that my boys hadn't. Within a month, however, that was over. As it happened, they had learned the same stuff, but didn't have the same vocabulary as the other kids. It didn't take long for them to associate the words with what they knew and to speak a common language.

The conceptual understanding is the hard part – the vocabulary to name it is easy.

What about college?

What about college? Will I hurt my child's chances at attending a good university by taking him out of school to travel?

That's a good question, and there is no pat answer.

If you, like my husband and I, feel that university is important and that you feel it's imperative that you prepare your child for university, then you'll need to make decisions with that in mind. You might choose your destinations carefully, picking sites where it will be easier to bring in more advanced topics. You might choose to carry more text books in the upper grades. You might opt to line up online tutors for subjects you aren't comfortable with.

I would say you don't have to think much about college until your child is 13 or 14 – just make sure that his basic skills are strong. Once he's capable of doing more advanced studies, you will need to consider other options.

There are several ways kids can enter college, so it's worth talking with a few universities to find out what their regulations are. One is to go through the regular application process, which can be difficult for children with atypical educations. The other is to take a year or two of classes at a community college or online, and then transfer into the university of choice. The latter route works well for roadschooled kids.

In the 'high school' years, many roadschoolers arrange for online classes, although that dictates their schedule more than other arrangements. Sometimes, kids are able to work through university material on their own.

The most important thing to say here is that roadschooling will not hold your child back or make it hard to succeed in university. You just need to be proactive and creative in figuring out the details.

Tips for enriching the experience

When you visit a new site, you basically have three options for how to deal with it:

1. Learn all you can before you get there
2. Research it after the visit
3. Don't dive deep at all; just learn what you can while there and then move on

Giving presentations to school groups or at senior centers is a great way for kids to show what they've learned.

Depending on the situation, all three of those approaches can be perfect. Overall, I would say our sons learned more when we researched a site beforehand. By the time we showed up in person, our boys knew a lot about how it all worked and why it was special. That then freed them up to move beyond the basics while at the site. They could talk with rangers and ask detailed questions to take their learning above and beyond. If they had arrived with no knowledge at all, they would have spent their time at the site learning the basics. Having a certain amount of prior knowledge allowed them to take it further.

Although the advance strategy is great, the truth is that it can't be done all the time. Sometimes you'll stumble upon a site that you didn't know existed and other times you are swamped and simply can't manage to do a bunch of research before visiting. That's when you have two choices.

You can choose to research after the fact. At the site, they learned the basics and now they can take it a step farther through research. Although we did this a number of times, we found it was harder than researching before because most websites only have the basic info. The rangers could get us further than internet research could. That said, if it's a fascinating site and you want to learn more, that's a way to take it to the next step.

Or you can choose to let it go. Accept that what you learned by visiting the site is enough and don't research it at all. There were times when we did that simply because a) we were too tired to bother studying at all or b) there was something else nearby that we found more interesting. It's all good.

A great strategy that is fun for many kids is to make models of monuments that you've visited. The models could be made of just about anything – from modeling clay to toothpicks – but the very act of recreating it cements it into kids' brains.

Oral presentations are another wonderful way for kids to take their learning to the next step. Can you find a nursing home that would enjoy hearing about your adventures? Or a school? Have each kid talk about something different to encourage them to dig deeper in their learning.

I would strongly encourage you to NOT go crazy with this. I recommend maybe three or four big units where you really dig deep per year – the last thing you want to do is to turn your child off to learning. Know that most of what you do in your travels will not become major learning units, and accept that for what it is. Choose the projects you want to dive into carefully, making sure they are topics that will be interesting to your children.

Be sure to keep it interesting and fun. Play with it. Have fun learning together.

Here are some ideas for projects to take learning to the next level:

-   Draw a picture
-   Act it out
-   Build a model
-   Write a story
-   Sing a song
-   Make a board game
-   Teach it to others
-   Write a letter to Grandma
-   Write a poem

Parental curiosity is key

All the research in the world won't help much if parents don't set the tone about learning. When we're excited and enthusiastic about learning something, our kids are too. When we're yawning and bored and want to head out, our kids pick up on that as well.

One of our most incredible learning experiences was sparked by my curiosity. We had seen small shrines on the side of the road since Mexico, but in Argentina we starting seeing some that were painted bright red. The red shrines all had red flags hanging from the tree above them. I was puzzled. Why red? What was the story?

As we sat on the side of the road taking breaks, I puzzled over the red shrines. Why? It didn't take long before my sons were curious too. As soon as we reached town, we researched and discovered a delightfully fascinating story about Gaucho Gil.

Parents set the stage for much of their children's learning. If you, as a parent, are interested in something, chances are your child will be as well.

My boys most likely never would have realized there were bright red shrines if it hadn't been for me bringing it up. It was my excitement and curiosity that drove them to wanting to learn about it. Keep your love of learning active and delve into what's around you. Your kids will do the same.

Gauchito Gil
Why are there red flags on roadside shrines in Argentina?

Throughout Argentina, you will find red shrines on the side of the road with red flags flying around them. These are shrines to Gaucho Gil. Although Gaucho Gil is not an official saint in the church, he is revered throughout the country of Argentina and is a 'defacto saint.'

Although there are many unknowns about Gaucho, we do know his full name was Antonio Mamerto Gil Nuñez. He is affectionately known as Gauchito Gil, and was born in the 1840's. He died January 8, 1878.

Gaucho was a deserter of the military who evaded capture for quite some time. During that time, he was a sort of 'Robin Hood' figure, robbing from the rich and giving to the poor.

When he was eventually captured and sentenced to death, he was hung upside down from a tree. As the executioner was preparing to behead him, Gaucho said, "Don't kill me - my pardon is coming. If you do kill me, your son will be stricken with a deadly illness, and the only way to save him will be to give my body a proper burial."

As expected, the executioner proceeded with his task and, when he arrived home, discovered that his son was deathly ill. He returned to the site of the execution and buried Gaucho's body. His son was miraculously cured and a legend was born.

Now, Argentineans have built shrines throughout the country to venerate the memory of Gaucho Gil. The significance of flags and red color are unknown, but may have something to do with either the color of Gaucho's political party or the color of the blood he shed.

Materials for Roadschooling

There are people out there who equate a mountain of teaching materials with a good education. Experience has shown, however, that you can provide an awesome education for your children with relatively few supplies. For roadschooling families with limited space, this fact is a godsend.

While I will be the first to admit that a good variety of teaching materials can make a teacher's life easier (much easier!) I've learned from my 21 years as a classroom teacher that they aren't necessary.

One year I walked into my new classroom in Albuquerque, New Mexico and quickly discovered a scene straight out of one of those horror films: it was empty. I had an empty teacher desk, a bunch of empty student desks, and a bookshelf filled with 200 copies of old fifth grade science and social studies books. I was teaching Grade 2 – 5 Special Education. I had nothing useable – not a single pencil nor piece of paper, no reading books or math books. Nothing. Nada. Zippo. Goose eggs.

And yet, I look back on that year now and marvel at the education my students received. I pulled out all the stops on that creativity box in my brain and we learned – a lot.

I made the rounds of travel agencies in town and picked up travel brochures for destinations around the globe. The kids and I cut out pictures of the seven continents and made collages. We wrote stories based on the pictures and used those as our reading materials. We sang songs and recited poems about various parts of the world. I went to a furniture store and rounded up refrigerator boxes to make dioramas. In short – those kids learned way more than they would have if I had had that mountain of teaching supplies at my fingertips.

As roadschoolers, we have the advantage of being in unique locations and we can take advantage of that fact. When you visit national parks, take time to listen to the ranger talks and read the info presented in the visitor centers. As you drive along the highway, stop and read the historical markers. You will find that a huge amount of your children's education can come from simply taking advantage of your local environment – wherever that happens to be today.

There are some materials that will make your life easier on the road. Each family will choose different items, but this is what we carried with us on our bicycles as we traveled the world on two wheels:

1. **Kindles** – the best purchase ever. Our sons could download English books no matter where we happened to be, and the Kindles took up very little space. They were way better than carrying lots of paper books.

2. **Math books** – For younger children, all they need to know in this area can easily be incorporated into your daily routine, but for older kids who are studying more advanced math, it's not as easy. We managed to get some math books from a school that had purchased new ones and was discarding their old copies.

3. **Notebook** – We had a notebook for each child. They used them as journals if we were camping out and they didn't have access to a computer, and also used them for math. We bought small notebooks and replaced them when full. If you will be doing a creative journal/scrapbook, you'll want larger ones.

4. **Calculator/Thesaurus/Dictionary/Translator** – One machine did it all. It was the size of a normal calculator, but was so much more.

5. **Maps** – We carried maps so we knew where we were going, but they also made great teaching materials.

Take advantage of your experiences, and you won't need many materials.

6. **Laptops and various CDs** – a computer is a great tool! We had a wide variety of educational programs for our children – from an entire earth science book that had been scanned to geography programs to math drills. There is no end to what you can find for the computer. In addition to CDs, there are wonderful programs to be found on the internet.

7. **Art supplies** – this was very limited on our bicycles, but if you have space it would be worth having a basic supply of art and craft stuff.

8. **Creativity** – This is the most important thing to take with you! By thinking creatively, you will find you can provide an incredible educational program for your children no matter where you happen to be in the world!

CASE STUDIES

Okay then, how do 'I' Roadschool? Where do I start?

Throughout this book, I've talked a lot about what we did – about how we built our sons' education into our daily life. However, each family's approach to roadschooling is as unique as that particular family.

Some families take a very organized approach and carefully plan out their destinations to mesh with what they want their children to learn. They may plan trips to historical sites, buy books about that period in history, and make an entire unit out of it. Other families have a more relaxed attitude about their child's education, believing he will learn what he needs to know from the experience of travel itself.

The important thing to remember is that there is no right and wrong. Do what feels comfortable and natural for both you, as parents, and for your children. My family used a variety of methods, depending on where we were, how much time we had, and what we wanted our children to learn. Other families stick to more routine.

The case studies presented in this section will introduce you to a number of roadschooling families. You will see that each family is unique, and they all take advantage of their experiences in their own way. Remember there is no right and no wrong, so pick what feels natural to you and leave the rest behind.

Every family handles education differently, and there is no right and wrong. Do what feels best for you.

Alisa Lybbert

Alisa Lybbert is a born adventurer who loves exploring the world with her (even more) adventurous husband, and their four young children, one of which is school age. She loves mountains, outdoor lifestyles, and she's positively crazy about veggies. Most of all, Alisa loves making memories with her family.

Alisa and her family lived in Mexico for two years, often touring the country in their minivan, and discovering the hidden jewels of Mexico, Guatemala and Belize. Most recently they spent a year exploring Europe, Southeast Asia, Indonesia, and the South Pacific with backpacks.

What is your basic educational philosophy? How do you see that kids learn?

Our educational philosophy is ever-changing and evolving as we constantly change our methods based on our children's needs. Our children learn very well with hands-on activities that come from our travels, but we felt that wasn't challenging them enough on a daily basis. For that reason, we've balanced what our children learn from our travels with online homeschool programs.

What do you envision for your children long-term in terms of education? University or no? Why do you think university is or is not important?

We expect our children to complete enough of a homeschool program that is equivalent of a high school degree (whether that be taking the GED or whatever is necessary at that point). We absolutely want our children to have the opportunity to go to university, if they choose.

I am a university graduate, and although I admittedly feel that my degree was a 'waste,' the experience of going to university was not. My husband went to a community college for several years, and was never a fan of school. I feel that he would have been the ideal personality type to have homeschooled, as he has an immense love of learning and researching, but does not appreciate being tested on it or put in group school settings.

Of course, the necessity of university depends on the child's professional interest. However, even if it is for the social opportunity of living on a campus and having roommates, I think it is of value to provide the circumstances for that opportunity.

What kind of preparation did you do before you hit the road?

We had no preparation, as our children were very young (ages 7 and 4 when we started). We carried a few small preschool books for our youngest daughter, but quickly ditched those. Both of our children had been in a private bilingual school in Mexico for 1 ½ years before we left on our indefinite-length trip. Our 7-year-old daughter would have been in 2nd grade the year we started out on the road. We purchased some pdf workbooks and had our older daughter work on those via the iPad, but also quickly abandoned that idea.

One of the best parts of roadschooling is being able to use our travels to further the education of our children. Can you give us an example of doing that?

It has been fun to give our children the opportunity to understand more concretely some aspects of the environment that they otherwise wouldn't. For example, our children have been hiking through gorges, and understand how water can cut through the rocks over thousands of years to make such beautiful places.

Also, in Southeast Asia they were given many opportunities to see and experience animals up close. We took them on an elephant-friendly tour in Thailand (i.e. a tour about healthcare of elephants and not just about entertaining tourists on an elephant ride) where they learned specifically how to inspect an elephant's health (through checking sweat glands on their toenails, reading the signs of their ears, inspecting how the elephants are sleeping, and checking to see if their poop is healthy). They learned about how elephants are at risk, and have become aware of animal exploitation. This is real tangible learning that they won't soon forget, unlike reading a book!

Although school and travel are intricately entwined and we're always working on our children's education, how much time do you spend daily or weekly on 'school stuff?' By that I mean the time spent directly on developing reading, writing, researching, math, or other skills typically taught in school.

It depends on the week and our current mode of travel. If we have planted ourselves in one spot, we try to get our (now 8) year old daughter to do about two hours of an online homeschool program per day. The program we're using is very thorough and covers all of the basic school subjects (math, language arts, science). It covers things I would never think of explaining to children, and really challenges them to think about word origins and such. It is very heavy on reading and phonetics, as well as math skills. It is also very thorough in explaining (in a fun and interactive way) a lot of concepts that I have found very difficult to approach with my daughter.

If we are traveling or sight-seeing that day, she skips the online program. At this age I often try to get her to write out her experiences in letters to family, but she is very resistant. As she grows older and more willing to write in a journal (without pulling teeth), I hope that we can get our older daughter to record her experiences and practice her handwriting skills that way.

Math has had a lot of real-life application. It's pretty easy to find opportunities to expand their math skills through daily activities, such as making purchases or dividing up things. Our daughter is also used to us throwing out multiplication and division facts, and she usually willingly takes on the challenge to answer them.

What educational materials do you carry with you?

We carry one reading/writing/math book for our daughter to work on. It is nice to have something that is not online for her to work on, since we don't always have internet access for her online programs. We also carry notepads, pencils, and crayons for other projects.

If you could give one piece of advice to a parent considering heading out to travel full time, what would it be?

It's not as scary to roadschool as you think. It's not about having the perfect plan *before* you begin your trip, but being willing to learn and adjust as you find what works for you while you are *on* your trip. Of course, this kind of advice is more suitable for families that will have internet access or the ability to change or add to what they have packed, and might not be as suitable for families on bikes.

We've discovered that children naturally want to learn, and every child has a different learning style. What may work for one child may not work for another. The important thing is having an open mind and being willing to listen to the needs and wants of your child, so you can find a learning path that is exciting and beneficial for him/her.

Read more about Alisa's adventures by visiting their website at www.livingoutsideofthebox.com.

Anne Van Loen

Anne Van Loen recently returned to Seattle, WA after spending thirteen months exploring the world together with her husband and two children (aged 13 and 11). Anne is an elementary school teacher and Noah a project manager. They planned for this big trip for about five years by reading books and family travel blogs, hosting an exchange student, spending less, and preparing for departure from home.

On their trip they spent time volunteering and learning Spanish in Peru, traveled by bus through Chile, trekked in Patagonia, hung out with big stone heads on Easter Island, road tripped through New Zealand, camped with Aussies, and snorkeled in the Great Barrier Reef. The New Year found the family visiting Myanmar (Burma), Bali, Malaysia, Cambodia, Thailand, Laos, and Vietnam. The trip wrapped up with adventures in China and Mongolia. Anne continues to homeschool both children.

What is your basic educational philosophy? How do you see that kids learn?

In my experience, people learn in dramatically different and equally valid ways. They thrive when given a magic mix of buy-in, challenge, and affirmation.

Learning can and should be messy at times. It involves taking risks and plenty of mistakes. Our ability to measure or 'see' that learning rests in a commitment to long-term relationships, natural observations, patience, and trust.

My preferred teaching style is experiential and project based. I believe that people learn by doing and by being fully engaged in the process. Instruction should be flexible; allowing for a range of interests and learning styles. Students should be encouraged to ask questions, seek answers themselves, and work with others towards a common goal.

I have always believed that children (all people, really) learn and grow naturally through play. I know some wonderful teachers who manage to engage their students in learning without making it all about 'work'. However, as children get older the time allowed for unstructured play tends to shrink dramatically. The nature of our trip and our daily lives has in many ways set us free of the 'fit it in' lifestyle, and we can reaffirm that play, work, and learning are far from mutually exclusive.

What do you envision for your children long-term in terms of education? University or no? Why do you think university is or is not important?

I don't have a plan for our children except that I plan to support their chosen path. Personally, I loved my college experience, especially my junior year abroad, and my kids know this. Do I think that a fancy degree is the ticket to future 'success' and happiness? Absolutely not. However, if one or both of them come to us with dreams and plans involving college, we will do our best to make it happen.

I think that the skyrocketing cost of universities these days make them considerably less of a good investment than they were in the past. Most parents can no longer afford to send their children to a four year college with the hope that they will use their time there to sort out what they want to be when they grow up. Travel, volunteering, employment, and internships seems to me a great alternative option to traditional college.

What kind of preparation did you do before you hit the road?

Before we left the states I researched the Washington State Homeschooling requirements and read a few blogs posted by other traveling families. I was already familiar with what fifth and seventh graders typically do in school so I wasn't really concerned.

One of the best parts of roadschooling is being able to use our travels to further the education of our children. Can you give us an example of doing that?

We started our trip in South America because I wanted to spend time living there and learning the language. Our first few weeks were really hard because sorting out the most basic daily tasks involved using our very beginning Spanish. We lived with a family for a month to avoid the temptations of seeking out other gringos and soon learned enough to read important signs, converse with taxi drivers, order from a menu, and arrange for laundry. The kids picked up many phrases and expressions that were NOT taught in our seven weeks of classes.

Living in Peru and interacting with the community in Cusco was by far the best natural teacher. We learned specific language skills while volunteering because we were in charge of a large group of children. Important statements such as: *siéntate!* (sit down!) *tranquilo!*(quiet!) *despacio!* (slow down!) *dame eso!* (give me that!) *buen trabajo* (great job!) *maravilloso!* (wonderful!) will stay with us! Both Alex and Leah were involved in teaching our English lessons and helped write and execute our bi-weekly plans. The local kids adored them and I think it was an even bigger learning experience for our kids to be the teacher

As expected, we faced some hardships as we traveled. I know that with each night spent sleeping on the floor, encounter with strangers, longer than expected hike, or mysterious food item - we grew. My worrying child especially has plenty of examples of how she made it through. We have found that we can laugh about what seemed so dark at the time and the incident quickly becomes part of family lore.

For us, newfound resilience and confidence come from dealing with disappointment, overcoming obstacles, and finding the joy (or at least the humor) in each day.

Although school and travel are intricately entwined and we're always working on our children's education, how much time do you spend daily or weekly on 'school stuff?' By that I mean the time spent directly on developing reading, writing, researching, math, or other skills typically taught in school.

The time we spent on traditional school type learning varied a great deal, depending on our circumstances. In general, it was no more than a couple hours a day when we were situated somewhere and dropped to nothing while we were on the move.

What educational materials do you carry with you?

Each child has a large ziplock bag. Included is a journal, a sketch pad, colored pencils, regular pencils, and a math workbook. We also travel with nooks and an iPad.

If you could give one piece of advice to a parent considering heading out to travel full time, what would it be?

Embrace your time away as exactly that. Don't try to run a mini-school on the road or worry that your children will fall behind academically. Instead, plan on being present, getting to know your children really well, and letting them teach and surprise you!

Amy Page

Amy, her husband, and four kids have been traveling since January 2010. Living in a caravan (RV) as they traveled Australia for four years, her family is now continuing their travels abroad. Amy and her husband share the homeschooling duties, often with Amy planning the activities for her husband to implement while she undertakes paid employment.

Traveling isn't their first experience at home educating their children; they spent three years homeschooling before they left their Melbourne home, but found they had to make changes to fit in with the ever-changing routine, lack of storage space, and weight restrictions that go with long-term travel. The experiences and challenges change as the children grow and develop, and the younger children begin to participate in formal education and the older children move on to new interests.

What is your basic educational philosophy? How do you see that kids learn?

It changes at different stages of their development. During the primary school years, I see it as fundamental that they learn or acquire four things: a love of learning, learning how to learn, reading and writing, and math.

A lot of the science and social science topics get incorporated into daily activities, literature, and travel at this age. It is about kindling the fire, not trying to stuff them full of information. Science, history and geography are a means to explain the world around them. That makes it relevant and memorable to young kids.

What do you envision for your children long-term in terms of education? University or no? Why do you think university is or is not important?

University is fundamental. I will accept it if my kids wish to do a trade, but I expect them to go to university. Even if they do not do a vocational degree (e.g. dentistry), it still opens doors that otherwise would be closed.

What kind of preparation did you do before you hit the road?

We were already homeschooling before we hit the road, so we made sure we took the curriculums we were using with us.

One of the best parts of roadschooling is being able to use our travels to further the education of our children. Can you give us an example of doing that?

We bought a 'podtour' on our way to Uluru (Ayer's Rock) in Central Australia. For three hours of driving through the desert, we listened to this fascinating tour telling us about the landscape, history, indigenous people, farming, and animals of the region. We reached Uluru with a greater understanding of it, and later when we drove from there to Kings Canyon, we listened to the next one in the series. While walking around Kings Canyon, we could connect the patterns on the rock that looked like the waves of the ocean, with the information that this area had been part of a massive inland ocean 300 million years ago.

We camped near Lake Eyre while it was in flood. This is a massive inland dry lake, which only fills about once every fifty years. We were there while it was flooded. My husband and kids went on a three hour joy flight over Lake Eyre to see the enormity and beauty of an inland lake, and on the way back they landed for afternoon tea at an abandoned Aboriginal mission.

Another time, we stopped at a ruined station for an afternoon, and walked around the buildings of this abandoned property, reading the history. The area had been discovered in the 1860s, during an unusually wet period. Of course, it had returned to drought, and the farmland was unprofitable. Reading about it in a book would have been quite dull, but walking around the empty sheering quarters, the derelict buildings, and crossing over the dry river bed with its great ghost gum trees to walk around their little cemetery made it real and memorable.

Although school and travel are intricately entwined and we're always working on our children's education, how much time do you spend daily or weekly on 'school stuff?' By that I mean the time spent directly on developing reading, writing, researching, math, or other skills typically taught in school.

We spend about two hours a day doing school.

What educational materials do you carry with you?

Each kid has a laptop and kindle, and they have an ipod that holds only audiobooks. We have phonics and spelling rules flashcards, and some math workbooks. Of course, we also have pens, pencils, paper, and books.

My older two children do online French lessons over Skype with a lady in France, and they do English lessons over Skype with a British lady. This makes a huge difference. I have a science background, but I feel that these two ladies do a better job of teaching these subjects formally than I could.

If you could give one piece of advice to a parent considering heading out to travel full time, what would it be?

The hardest part is going. Sometimes I question if the kids would be more advanced in math and English if we had stayed at home, but I know they have an appreciation and knowledge that goes beyond that.

Learn more about the Page family by visiting them on the web at www.livinontheroad.com.au.

Annie André

Annie André is an experienced traveler and ex-corporate lackey who, together with her husband and three children decided to take the road less traveled and leave the American dream behind to live in France for a few years.

Annie was born in Thailand to a Thai mother and French Canadian father and raised in three countries. Over the course of her life, she traveled and/or lived abroad as a child, a teenager, a young adult and now as a wife and mother of three in the south of France.

Although living in France had always been a dream of theirs, they never actually believed it was something they could achieve any time soon due to being tied to their jobs and life in California by golden handcuffs.

Then the economy took a turn and they BOTH got laid off on the same day. After a long bout of unemployment, something clicked, (probably the sound of those golden handcuffs coming off). That's when they decided to take the road less travelled and do the unthinkable.

They decided to rebuild their life the way they wanted it to look rather than the way society told them it was supposed to look.

What is your basic educational philosophy? How do you see that kids learn?

My eyes have been opened to various methods of teaching and learning ever since we left the comfort of our suburban life in the San Francisco Bay area behind.

As a result, my basic educational philosophy has evolved over the course of the last three years to what it is today which is the following:

- I believe that some kids (my kids) need the structure of a classroom but that they also need to be allowed to explore their creativity, talents and passions that the structured environment of school does not give them.

- I achieve this by using a hybrid method of learning and teaching my children. I combine traditional schooling (public French school) with home/world schooling.

- At school, they are immersed in French language, culture, and their French friends.

- At home, I take cues from my children and explore their interests, talents, and passions that they cannot explore at school.

For instance, my 15-year-old son has an interest in drawing and 3D animation. I have created a curriculum for him around this interest and shaped it in such a way that if he wanted to, he could possibly pursue this as a career choice. He takes online classes, is creating a website to showcase his work, and I am exploring with him different options for careers that he might like to do based on his interests.

I think by using this hybrid method, it gives them a broader and well-rounded education. They understand how to function in a world where they need to adhere to certain guidelines to survive while also following their talents, interests and passions that may one day become their career choice.

What do you envision for your children long-term in terms of education? University or no? Why do you think university is or is not important?

I used to think that university WAS THE ONLY way to get ahead in life no matter what your career and life goals but as I mentioned earlier, my educational philosophy has changed and I no longer believe that for several reasons.

- Some people, like my middle child, just don't learn well in a classroom setting. No matter how much he loves the subject matter he has a hard time focusing and I can't see him sitting through a bunch of university classes that don't interest him just because they are part of the university curriculum. Unless something changes, he will most likely not go to university. Instead I am encouraging him to hack his education now by turning his raw talents and interests into a potential career. As of now that could be 3D animation or cooking. Who knows?

- I don't think it makes sense to rack up a $50,000 or even a $20,000 debt just to go to school if it means that you have to carry that debt over the course of the next ten and, in some cases, twenty years. I think there are better ways to hack your education.

I understand that some careers absolutely require you to get a degree, like doctors and lawyers but those typically have the salary to match after graduation so that they can pay back their student loans. My eldest son does learn well in a classroom setting and is definitely going to attend university after taking a gap year to travel and work.

What kind of preparation did you do before you hit the road?

We did no preparation whatsoever and this was one of our biggest mistakes.

You've said that your attempts at roadschooling failed. How so? What happened?

When we left California back in August of 2010, we thought we would be homeschooling for no more than two months. My plan was to just maintain math and English during that time.

BACKSTORY: Originally, we planned on moving from California to the east coast. Neither myself nor my husband had jobs waiting for us so we set up a home base with my aunt in Montreal. The plan was to live there for a few months until my husband found a job. Once he found one, we would then rent a home near that job and put the kids back in school. After a few months we realized that perhaps we would not be able to find jobs and our plans literally changed overnight.

We decided to take the road less travelled and go to France with the kids to give them French fluency, expose them to another culture and at the same time be home for them while my husband and I worked on our personal and freelance goals.

This sudden change in plans meant that we had to homeschool the boys for longer than I anticipated until we could get visas to move to France. (It took us eight months to get visas).

My biggest mistake at that point was not reaching out to other homeschoolers for direction and help. I was still stuck on this idea that I had to home school them the same way that they would be schooled in a traditional setting.

We focused on reading, writing, math and history but the idea of making it fun for them just never occurred to me. That's just not the way I was taught and back in California I did not know anyone who homeschooled.

To make matters worse, we had just ripped our children from a very comfortable life in the San Francisco bay area where they attended school and had loads of friends.

Everything seemed so hard and my relationship with my boys started to suffer really badly. We were crying almost every day and arguing almost every day. It was literally hell for all of us.

For the sake of my relationship with my boys, I decided to let up on their home schooling.

We let their homeschooling follow a more natural path which I know today to be a form of 'un-schooling.' We decided to let them focus on their artistic endeavors. Our reasoning was that it was temporary and that eventually they would have to get back to the basics and go back to public school.

Kieran focused on guitar and Andre focused on drawing. My aunt in Montreal who is Francophone even helped out and gave my two sons French lessons everyday which they seemed to like a lot because it wasn't me yelling at them anymore.

That's when I began to see that it wasn't the end of the world if they did not follow the traditional method or timeline of learning. That's when my educational philosophy began to change.

I still have old school beliefs about how I want my children to learn but I have a more open mind to other ways of learning now. Roadschooling and homeschooling are amongst those methods.

One of the best parts of roadschooling is being able to use our travels to further the education of our children. Can you give us an example of doing that?

While in France and travelling around Europe, we always take advantage of upcoming trips to expand our children's knowledge of the world.

For instance, before going to Berlin, we piqued our children's interest in German history by showing them movies about the great wall, the holocaust, and Germany. This set the stage for the next level of learning. We asked our two older boys to do some research on Germany and Berlin and then pick a few places that they learned about to visit.

We have found that by doing this, they are more engaged and genuinely more interested in the places we visit.

Usually, when we return home, they either continue learning on their own or move on to the next thing.

Through this method, we have discovered that one of our kids, the eldest, is very interested in politics. My other son, who we thought had NO interests besides video games, started showing an interest in foods of the world.

Although school and travel are intricately entwined and we're always working on our children's education, how much time did you spend daily or weekly on 'school stuff?' By that I mean the time spent directly on developing reading, writing, researching, math, or other skills typically taught in school.

When we strictly homeschooled, we spent about two hours a day on school related stuff and then the kids spent about two hours on self-directed studies.

What educational materials did you carry with you?

We carried history, literature and math books with us which we bought from a used bookstore selling homeschooling material in Maryland.

If you could give one piece of advice to a parent considering heading out to travel full time, what would it be?

Our biggest mistake in homeschooling was to try and replicate how school is taught in a traditional classroom setting. Instead, I suggest you start slow and develop your own curriculum and go at you and your child's pace. Choose courses based on his or her interests too. Kids learn better when it's fun and not forced.

Follow the André family by visiting www.annieandre.com.

Connie Perry

Connie Perry spent eighteen months roadschooling her 9-year-old twins as they toured the USA visiting state capitols. She has a degree in elementary education and a minor in early childhood education.

Before leaving on their great adventure, she was a full-time mom, part-time enrichment teacher and part-time consulting head teacher for a nursery school.

What is your basic educational philosophy? How do you see that kids learn?

My hope is that my children will be lifelong learners, and we do use a formal curriculum. I was a preschool enrichment teacher before we hit the road, so my style may be a bit more formal than others. I try to use formal teaching and life experiences. Our curriculum provides a test at the end of every twenty lessons which we take, but it is more important to me to see my children use their knowledge in everyday situations. They love to tell people we meet about the things they have learned.

What do you envision for your children long-term in terms of education? University or no? Why do you think university is or is not important?

My husband and I both have college degrees. He has an MBA and I have a few masters credits. If he did not have a good job for the last fifteen years we would not have felt as comfortable taking this leap of faith (selling most everything to travel and work on the road.)

However, this journey has taught us life isn't about the money. It is about spending time with your children and not rushing around to every possible activity. I guess ultimately if our children found a way to support themselves with something they enjoy doing it would not matter if they went to college. On the other hand it is nice not to have to worry so much about money.

What kind of preparation did you do before you hit the road?

We withdrew from the school system in the middle of the school year so I met with my daughter's teacher who had been teaching for over thirty years. I wanted to just expand and continue what they had been learning. My son's teacher was a first time teacher, but was glad to share any information he could.

I bought the same math workbooks (used on ebay) that they had been using in school. For the first four months I used book store workbooks for spelling, reading, and phonics.

When it was time for 3rd grade I decided I wanted a curriculum. I like formal learning and that is all my children have ever known. I enjoy teaching when things are connected spelling/reading/phonics.

I purchased a used curriculum as I really like to reuse anything I can. I think this world already has so much trash. I did purchase extra copies of the workbooks so they each would have one. I felt the curriculum was challenging and connected to what we were seeing in the real world. I don't think you will know what exactly works for you until you try it.

One of the best parts of roadschooling is being able to use our travels to further the education of our children. Can you give us an example of doing that?

I definitely think History, Science, Reading and Math lend themselves to roadschooling best.

The idea of visiting the capitols of each state started long before we had children. When I was in fourth grade, I had to learn the states and their capital cities, but...well, I didn't. For the rest of my life I could never remember the capitols. After my husband and I visited Boston, I decided I wanted to set the goal of visiting all the state capitols so I could make a connection to them and remember them.

We had read about Nathan Hale and his famous last words, "I regret I have one life to give for my country." When we toured the capitol in Connecticut, we saw his statue. We then found directions to the schoolhouse where he began his teaching career.

I think we learn best when we can make a connection. At capitols we also learn about architecture, something I knew little about. My children enjoy taking the tours of the capitols and sometimes we learn history, government, economics, art, geography or architecture during the tours. In Jefferson City, MO the tour guide pointed out a painting of a bridge in St Louis which, when viewed from one direction showed one perspective, and a different perspective when viewed from a different direction. When we got to St. Louis we were sure to walk across the bridge and compare it to the painting. I will remember that for a long time because of the connection we were able to make.

National parks also make our list of great places to educate. In Yellowstone we attended a ranger talk on bears where we learned the difference between black and grizzly bears. We also attended a talk on coyotes and learned how they are like us.

We always get the Junior Ranger Program information at national parks, which are extremely educational. I encourage my kids to do the activities, but they are not required to. They always want to finish them. For me it is not about getting the badge it is about learning about and feeling connected to the place we are right at that time. I also love to watch the films at the national parks as they are well done and always seem to put everything we learn into perspective.

In history we were studying about famous Americans. When we were in the east we toured Civil War battlegrounds. I started my children's studies with Gettysburg and a book on how to be a Civil War soldier. The book mentioned many important battles and my son especially loved it. We planned our travels to go to where the war started, where it ended, and many of the battlefields in between. We learned about the important generals in each battle as well.

My daughter wanted to read a book about Seaman, the dog who traveled with Lewis and Clark across the country, after she noticed the book in Washington DC. That is another suggestion I have – let your children choose books that interest them at national parks. We have especially noticed stops on our trip where Lewis and Clark (and Seaman) had been. We saw a film about them at the St. Louis arch, talked about them as we crossed the Missouri and we were excited to go to Fort Clatsop to see where they spent the winter. Lewis, Clark and Sacajawea were also in our history book, but we were more connected because we followed their path and talked about them many times.

As for math, my children are learning firsthand about how much things cost. We keep a record of what we pay for gas and campgrounds. They learn about miles per gallon and miles per hour. Sometimes they follow along with a map as we travel.

Although school and travel are intricately entwined and we're always working on our children's education, how much time do you spend daily or weekly on 'school stuff?' By that I mean the time spent directly on developing reading, writing, researching, math, or other skills typically taught in school.

We usually do about three hours of formal school work at a time. On days that we travel, I sit between them in the RV and they do work. I am very lucky that they do not get car sick and I actually miss it when we do not have work to do, as it makes the time go faster. We may do school work six days a week (we always take Sunday off) and then when we are busy we may not do it at all.

Their grandmothers each travel to visit us about every two months and we don't do any school work when we are with them. Our curriculum has 176 days of lessons which took us 9-10 months to complete. We are taking a month off before we start fourth grade, but we still do multiplication and division review and write in our 'what I saw' journals almost every day.

What educational materials do you carry with you?

Lots and lots of books! My daughter reads two, three, or even four books a day when we are not doing school work. We frequent thrift stores and used book stores to stock up. I also have a crate in which I store their curriculum (lesson manuals, math book, math workbook, history, science, phonics, reading, spelling, vocabulary, geography and grammar.) Our curriculum also has an art appreciation section.

If you could give one piece of advice to a parent considering heading out to travel full time, what would it be?

Don't stress too much about roadschooling; I think I over-stressed. As we were traveling, it all fell into place. If you are a structured person like I am, you probably should buy a curriculum as it puts all the pieces in place so you can just concentrate on teaching. I have also learned not to judge others. Some people school more and some school less. Each family needs to find what flows best for them

To learn more about this family, visit them on the web at unpredictableperrys.wordpress.com

Hannah Miller

Hannah is one half of a mother/daughter team represented here in this book – she's the daughter part. Hannah is a seventeen year old writer and musician with a serious case of wanderlust. Over the past few years she's traveled to over twenty-four countries, on five different continents, using bikes, buses, trains, planes, and of course, her own two feet. Wherever she goes, a video camera and three instruments follow.

Tell me about your education. What kinds of things do you do that you consider 'schooling' or 'education.'

As far as schooling goes, we've always been relatively traditional, in that my parents firmly believe in using curriculums and textbooks. We each use a variety of textbooks and/or online programs that have been hand-selected to suit our own particular learning styles. I've taken higher math, history, literature, geography, sciences, and arts.

Because I learn best through written material, many of my courses have included textbooks. However, I've also listened to college lectures on a variety of subjects with a program called the Great Courses.

What are your goals for your education? Do you hope to go to university? In a perfect world, what would these years of your childhood prepare you for?

I actually had completed most of my high school work by the time I was fifteen, and am currently enrolled online at Oregon State University as a non-degree seeking student. Next year, I intend to transfer to Queens University, in Canada, where I'd like to get a degree in Geography. I'm passionate about helping those in need around the world, with a particular focus towards breaking the cycle of poverty in Guatemala. At the moment, I'm taking classes that should help me to work with teachers, kids, and organizations that are working towards similar goals.

This is by no means a perfect world, but I think that if I hadn't had travel as a significant part of my education I almost certainly would not be as passionate about the education/poverty cycle that we see in so many developing countries. Traveling has not only opened my eyes to these issues in a way nothing else really could, it's actually prepared me to deal with them. Because I've been exposed to many different cultures from an early age, I'm comfortable around them. I know how to communicate when no one speaks my language. It's probably much easier for me to operate in a foreign country than it would be for someone who's new to international travel.

When most people think of school, they think of the 3 R's – Reading, wRiting, and 'Rithmetic. Do you consider that you are below average, average, or above average in those three areas? In other words, do you think you know about as much as kids in traditional educational settings in the basic 3 R's?

Among my peer group I've tested as above average in all three of those. One of the great benefits of homeschooling is that students are allowed to work at their own pace. If I didn't understand something right away, I could take extra time to really make sure that I had learned the material thoroughly. Also, since I finished high school two years early, I've had plenty of time to move forward.

In what ways do you think your education differs from those in more traditional environments? In which ways is it better? In which ways is it worse?

Since we're often on the road, the actual hours that I work on school tend to be pretty flexible. I think one of the upsides to our method of education is that I'm allowed to manage my own schedule to some degree. This allows me to work in my peak hours and learn things as quickly or as slowly as I need to. When I was younger my parents did monitor how fast I was working through the material, because I had pretty terrible time management skills at that point. But now it's my own responsibility, and I really enjoy that.

The other main upside to roadschooling is, obviously, the travel. I love being able to come into contact with other cultures and ways of life. Every day is a new adventure, and it keeps me eager to learn new things.

The downsides are the long periods of time away from family and friends, and that very rarely do you find anyone who has had many of the experiences you've had. I've learned to connect with people from all walks of life, but it's pretty uncommon for me to find others who understand what being raised on the road is like and can swap stories and laugh about that one god-awful bus ride everyone can relate to. When I do meet other kids who 'get it' we tend to bond pretty quickly.

But with the internet, those things are becoming less of an issue. We Skype with our friends and family back home as often as we can, and I've made quite a few friends who've also been raised on the road through online classes and forums. I've got buddies on every inhabitable continent at the moment, which is pretty cool!

Think long term – think of yourself as a young adult entering the work force. How do you think your experiences being roadschooled will set you apart from others?

I know that international experience is becoming ever more important to have on your resume. As technology is becoming more advanced, the world is getting smaller. Businesses are looking for people who can comfortably interact with many different social and ethnic groups. They're also looking for people with good leadership and problem solving skills. Travel has a tendency to give you those skills. Having been raised on the road, I have the advantage of having tons of international experience already, as well as the leadership and problem solving skills that come with it. Hopefully that will help me to stand out from the crowd.

What advice would you give a parent who is considering traveling and roadschooling her children?

Be brave. I know that many people have the tendency to be really scared or nervous about committing to roadschooling their kids. Don't be. Once you commit to doing it, it'll all start to come together. The things you're afraid of suddenly won't seem half as bad, and before you know it you'll be living your dreams.

I think everyone has a tendency to feel nervous before the start of a new adventure. I still feel that way occasionally, and we've been traveling for years! Oddly enough, I was nervous about coming home just a few weeks ago. But it's important not to let your fears hold you back from doing the thing you want to do, whether that be travel or something else entirely. So be brave! Knuckle down and make it happen!

Visit Hannah on the web at www.edventuregirl.com.

Jenn Miller

Jenn Miller is the mama in this mother/daughter pair. She is gypsy mama to four wild adventurer children growing up with the world as their classroom. The Miller family is in their sixth year of an open ended world tour that has taken them through about thirty countries so far. They've journeyed across Europe and N. Africa on bicycles, the length and breadth of North and Central America, deep instead of wide for six months in Guatemala, seven months across mountains and rivers across Southeast Asia and they've backpacked their way through Borneo and Indonesia and thoroughly road tripped Australia and New Zealand.

When she's not hiking in rain forests or SCUBA diving remote islands in Belize, Jenn can be found riding off into the sunset with Arab horsemen or swing dancing under the stars on her favorite Iago with her husband of twenty years and lifelong adventure buddy.

What are your goals in terms of roadschooling. What do you hope to accomplish?

Our goal, in general, is to provide a thorough and rigorous education for our children that will prepare them for whatever their later goals in life might be. Roadschooling is one aspect of that ongoing project. We have always schooled our children outside the institutional system, so learning while we travel was not an adjustment we had to make in their educational program; it was just the natural outgrowth of our travels. Adding travel to the 3R's provides a depth and context for many of the traditional subjects that isn't possible within the context of a more traditional learning environment.

What kind of preparation did you do (in terms of education) before you hit the road?

When we began traveling we intended to be gone for just one year, two at most. We prepared our kids, educationally, for that period of time 'off' of their core academic subjects by working ahead in math so that we were confident they would not be 'behind' when we returned. We needn't have worried. They all tested at or above grade level at the end of that first year, even with no formal 'book time' during our cycle trip.

When we made the decision to keep traveling, we adjusted our educational plans to allow for a balance of academic subjects and free-form 'on the road' style learning.

Tell us about your schedule. What role does your children's education play in your daily life on the road?

We work to strike a balance between a rigorous intellectual education and a thorough 'real world' education for our children. The structure that works best for our family is to use mornings for 'book work' and afternoons for adventures. Of course flexibility is key as there are times when we're stationary and can really dig into project style learning and deeper research, and there are other times when we're road tripping or otherwise moving forward and our book work takes a back seat to the many things there are to learn all around us.

Our kids are now 11, 13, 15 & 17. Our youngest beginning his middle-school work and our oldest is in her second year of university classes online. They are largely responsible for their own course work and scheduling. It's fantastic for them to be growing up in this era with technology supporting alternative lifestyles in a way that allows them to have the best of both worlds.

Although education and travel are intricately entwined and we're always working on our children's education, how much time do you spend daily or weekly on 'school stuff?' By that I mean the time spent directly on developing reading, writing, researching, math, or other skills typically taught in school.

The time the kids spend on 'school work' varies by age. Our youngest spends 2-3 hours a day on his sixth grade book work. My high school level sons spend about four hours. Hannah's university classes vary greatly depending on which courses she's taking and the level of interaction required online. It's up to them to accomplish the agreed upon content for the year, week by week, according to the plans we've made.

We incentivize diligence and efficiency, so it's in their best interest to knock it out of a morning and get on with their other projects. I should also mention that we only school four days per week. It never seemed to me that kids needed a five day per week job, so we set up our academic calendar and plans to take Wednesdays off. This has leant a great deal of flexibility to our schedule that serves us well when we're traveling.

What educational materials do you carry with you?

We carry three computers (one each for the older children and one for the younger boys to share) and an iPad that is shared, each child has an ipod and we have two e-readers that are shared. Many of their courses are computer based, or we put the DVD portions onto their hard drives so that there's less to carry.

Most of the paperwork that they need is printable on an 'as needed' basis, so we're rarely carrying more than a small notebook of materials for each child at a time. We're so thankful for the myriad of resources available online and as e-downloads.

When we began traveling, in 2008, it was much more difficult because e-publishing was in its infancy and there were not a lot of e-books available for children yet and the digital textbook revolution hadn't exploded. We carried a lot more paper books back then! Now, virtually everything is digital and our kids read on their ipods and computers.

One of the best parts of roadschooling is being able to use our travels to further the education of our children. Can you give us an example of doing that?

We spent much of last year exploring Southeast Asia, based in Thailand. Before we took off for Vietnam we spent about two months studying the Vietnam War intensively: reading books, watching documentaries, exploring the history and politics of both sides of the conflict. When we got to Vietnam we toured Ho-Chi-Minh's headquarters and the prison that housed American POWs and anti-communist collaborators. We took motorcycle rides up into the hills to examine the remaining US bunkers above the Perfume River and spent the day talking to our guide, the son of a man who died on the Vietnamese side of the conflict.

Because of our prior research, the children had a deeper understanding of what they were seeing. They were able to ask deeper questions and see the propaganda on both sides for what it was instead of just dropping into a place 'cold' with little background or context for what they experienced. The whole purpose of our travels is to support the educational process of our children. It's an elaborate field trip, if you will, to deepen their understanding beyond the book learning that is also important.

Of course our children journal and do currency conversions as we go, which lend a practical usefulness to basic numeracy and the ability to write; those sorts of connections are obvious. They've also had art lessons from a Vietnamese brush painter, music lessons from a range of talented travelers and performers we've encountered in various places, plien-aire drawing and painting sessions at Uluru, Angkor Wat and ruin sites across Central America, as well as study sessions in the great art museums of Europe. Immersion Spanish lessons in

Guatemala yielded much better (and faster!) results than any of the 'programs' we'd employed previously.

History, science, literature and geographical studies are easily woven in according to where we find ourselves in any given month. I make the effort to think about that ahead of time and design educational experiences as jumping off points for the learning that's taking place quite naturally every day. It's really just a matter of being present enough in your thought process as a parent and an educator to consider what educational resources you have at hand and find a way to light that fire of interest in your child to want to know more, whether you're traveling or not.

Are you concerned about university? If so, what are you doing to make sure your children are ready? If not, then ignore this question.

We are definitely concerned about university! In our family, university is viewed as the completion of a basic education. We expect that each of our children will get a bachelor's degree, at least. Not because we expect them to get nine to five jobs and participate in the economic machine, necessarily, but because we want to equip them to pursue whatever they want to in life and a university degree is another tool that they can use to further their life goals.

Our daughter is already working on her university work online. We expect that our children will get their degrees creatively, and at a lower financial cost than the traditional paths. We expect our kids to continue with a university degree because it adds depth to their understanding of the world and fuels their passions in life. In our family, employment is not the expected ends of education, and a university degree, along with all other intellectual education provides "delight, ornament & ability" as Charlotte Mason would say, for a well-rounded life.

If you could give one piece of advice to a parent considering heading out to travel full time, what would it be?

Chase hard after your dream, and take your kids with you. I think the most important lessons we impart, without saying a word, to our children are those that grow out of a passion driven life: perseverance, joy in the journey, intentional living, work to support lifestyle, creativity, determination and not settling for less than your personal best.

Kids raised with passion-driven parents gain a belief that anything is possible, and the understanding of the work that it takes to make that 'anything' happen. Those are gifts that keep on giving, for generations into the future. Organizing an above-average intellectual education for your child in an outside the box way is the easy part. It's those deeper lessons about life and how to live it that are priceless and are facilitated by living life your way.

Visit the Millers on the web at www.edventureproject.com.

Kimberly Travaglino

Kimberly Travaglino is anything but sane. Wife to Chris, mom to four exuberant kiddos, roadschool mom, author, radio show personality, blogger, editor in chief and digital gypsy, she's still trying to figure out what she wants to be when she grows up!

The one thing she doesn't have to decide is where she wants to live. For the past three years, the Traveling Travaglinos have lived everywhere.

When we first started roadschooling, it was a small part of a series of life changes. We had just had our fourth baby, my husband had just quit his corporate job and was looking for his place as a stay at home dad and we had just traded our 3500 square foot home for a 350 foot fifth wheel, parked in the Florida Everglades, in July.

We were miserable, but I was so full of Type A angst that it never occurred to me to go slow, let ourselves adjust, and take a break (it was, after all, July!). I felt this enormous pressure from friends and family alike to not let my kids lose any ground.

I should tell you that at that time, we had a 1st grader, a Kindergartner, a preschooler and a newborn.
Looking back now, I know I was crazy. I wished someone had told me it was all going to be okay. Stressing out was not necessary – and not at all conducive to learning. If someone did tell me, I wished I had listened. I had done so much research on the 'right way' to roadschool and I wanted to make sure I capitalized on our travels. I wanted desperately for our kids to understand the concepts and history behind the places we were visiting.

But if you want to know the absolute truth, lean in a little closer, I'm going to share a secret with you... I didn't know the concepts and history behind the places we were visiting.

Case in point, one of our first stops was Jamestown, Virginia. I had no idea what that place was about. I recognized Pocahontas' name, but only because I had seen the Disney movie. Chris and I picked up the Junior Ranger programs (under the auspices of helping the kids) and filled in the entire booklets. We left as brand new colonial experts.

That was an eye opener. I knew from that point forward, that Chris and I were the ones who were really digesting the lessons – the true learners. But I also realized it was the light foundation of history, science, social studies that I learned in my formative years that allowed me to assimilate the experiences we were having into true knowledge.

From that moment forward, my goal for educating the kids was to expose them to the history, the ideas. Give them some back story, and let them distill the information in whatever way made sense to them, individually.

I realized that I didn't want to emulate school, or try to recreate it in the camper; my goal was to teach them how to learn. Give them the tools to look things up. Introduce them to Google and Wikipedia. And most importantly teach them to be curious.

So what do the lessons I refer to above look like on a daily basis in our camper.

We start school after breakfast. We work on math daily, working through a Saxon workbook appropriate for their levels. Then it's a spelling list, penmanship, and a history workbook that's one page narrative, the other page reinforcing puzzle. After they get those things done, they read for one hour each.
Some days we don't do school at all. We might take a field trip, or we just might hang out. We do school all year round, mostly because we don't know what month it is.

What effect has this type of education had on my children? Unlike their brick and mortar schooled counterparts, they are learning to be daring, adventurous risk takers. They are learning that to find out what something does or how something works, it's way better to poke it with a stick than to read about it in some dusty book (exception to this rule is anything venomous).

They are learning that the basics are necessary and that discipline is rewarded, but that delayed gratification does not mean you have to delay living until the age of retirement rolls around.

Most importantly, they are learning that life is what you make it, and we are currently making it beautiful!

To learn more about this extraordinarily family, visit them on the web at www.fulltimefamilies.com.

Mary Hickox

Mary is a unschooling mom to three boys. She has home-schooled, unschooled, and roadschooled her boys as they have made the leap to fulfill their dreams of ultimate freedom through travel. They left the US seven years ago to live as expats in Costa Rica and two years ago left for a nomadic lifestyle traveling through Asia and Australia nonstop. They are now loving life in Hawaii where learning is an adventure around every corner.

What is your basic educational philosophy? How do you see that kids learn?

I hate to use labels but they are typically the best way to explain your position quickly. We unschool our boys. They learn what they are interested in and in a normal everyday environment rather than at a school desk. But even though they do not 'do' school, they still learn every day. They learn while we live our life, doing chores, exploring the world through travel, and through the constant family conversations that we have.

What do you envision for your children long-term in terms of education? University or no? Why do you think university is or is not important?

In terms of long term I see my boys doing what speaks to them. I know that sounds cheesy but it is honestly the way we see it. If they want to or need to attend university then that is wonderful and we will support them, but they also understand that it is not the only path to take.

I would be surprised if they all went to college and, truthfully, I do not care if they do or not; I just want them to make the decision based on what they love and are happy doing, not because society or their parents think they should.

I cannot say that university is or is not important overall. In some instances it is very important and a useful thing to do, but for many people it is simply unnecessary and only leads to a mound of debt. If they need it to pursue their passion then it is very important, but only if it helps them reach a goal.

What kind of preparation did you do before you hit the road?

None really, we just live our life and learn as we go. You really cannot stop a person from learning; it happens every day in nearly every moment. For us we just learn all the time so no need to prepare for that. I do research every place we travel to extensively and we chat about it often, we have all learned loads from that!

One of the best parts of roadschooling is being able to use our travels to further the education of our children. Can you give us an example of doing that?

There are loads of examples of this; nearly every day is a learning adventure of some kind. A great specific example is when we went to Angkor Wat in Cambodia. We spent days together researching Cambodia in general before we went, using math to work out the money conversion. We talked about the geography of the area and planned which temples we wanted to see inside the grounds.Our oldest sons both read online and chose what looked best.

While there, we drew sketches of the temples we were viewing and chatted about what it must have been like to live when it was a thriving city, as well as how awful it must have been during the 80's when Pol Pot's men nearly ruined it.

In that one week we all learned geography, history, theology, math, reading, and more. It was amazing but not unlike any other week. This week we went snorkeling, hung out with turtles, and saw rainbow after rainbow. We always discuss these things and go back home and research together any concept we do not understand. Science, history, and loads of reading are just part of a travel life.

Although school and travel are intricately entwined and we're always working on our children's education, how much time do you spend daily or weekly on 'school stuff?' By that I mean the time spent directly on developing reading, writing, researching, math, or other skills typically taught in school.

Again this is a hard one to nail down. We learn all the time and don't separate learning from living, so I cannot really say how many hours in any given week. I almost never sit down and make them write or read or anything like that unless they ask me to.

That being said, we are always reading together (not much writing) but they do type a lot. Math happens all the time and when it intertwines with life we go with it and deepen their knowledge. Travel research does take up several hours a week and we all learn from that. Things like geography, languages, history, culture, and science are covered intensely during that time.

What educational materials do you carry with you?

We have books, of course, and we also utilize electronics (Kindle, laptops, ipad) as we are limited to what we can carry. We have a few workbooks that we carry around as well as basic art supplies so that when the kids want to use them they can. When we stay someplace for more than a couple weeks we add more art supplies or musical instruments to the arsenal.

If you could give one piece of advice to a parent considering heading out to travel full time, what would it be?

My best advice and it applies to every facet of life and travel, is to just relax. Enjoy every moment and appreciate the experiences good and bad. People spend so much time worrying and stressing that they lose part of their life experience in doing so.

You need to be sure that your children can function in society but it is unnecessary to stress about each and every little thing that happens in school. Travel will give them an education they could never get in school. Let go and live, you'll be surprised how much learning happens just in that!

To learn more about the Hickox family visit them on the web at www.bohemiantravelers.com.

Paige Conner Totaro

Former (recovering?) lawyer, Paige has recently returned from an 11-month trip around the world with her husband and twin 13-year-old daughters and is already planning the next adventure. As a travel consultant and blogger, Paige hopes to inspire people to explore new cultures, learn new languages, and make friends around the world.

What is your basic educational philosophy? How do you see that kids learn?

We are not lifelong homeschoolers; we homeschooled only for the year that we were traveling. I have a great faith that schools and teachers, who have been trained to teach our kids, do a better job than I could overall. I do believe that school is not the best fit for everyone, and that kids are quite capable of learning outside of the classroom.

Every kid learns differently. I have twin daughters who have completely differently ways of learning. One is utterly self-directed, disciplined, and a perfectionist. The other is bright, but not really interested in school. They both love reading, languages, and art.

Our homeschooling experience taught us a great deal about our kids. We were surprised to see that when she was responsible for her own math learning, our less-motivated child worked much harder to understand the concepts than she ever had in school. That taught us that we should give her more control over her learning, while giving her specific goals to work toward.

I believe you should play to your strengths, and we try to help our kids do this, too. Where they have a natural proclivity for something, we let them shine, but with things that are tougher, we try not to harp too much. It took us a while to reach this point, though. When one of our daughters struggled in math, our instinct was to push her harder, until a math teacher told us that some math concepts are developmental in nature, meaning that you really can't make a child learn them until they're ready. It made for a much happier household when we backed off and let her switch to a less advanced course level.

What do you envision for your children long-term in terms of education? University or no? Why do you think university is or is not important?

Since both my husband and I went to college, the assumption is that our kids will, too. But I've been thinking a lot about this lately, as we approach the high school and college years. I absolutely believe that if a kid has a specific career in mind, and she can find a college that offers a good program of study at a reasonable price, she should go for it (though I do believe a gap year of travel can do nothing but add to the experience).

If a kid is unsure about a career path, and doesn't love learning for the sake of learning, then maybe college is not the place for them at age 18. Or if a kid is ready for a career path or life experience right out of high school, maybe college would be a waste of time for them. Think of entrepreneurs like Steve Jobs who really would not have gained much, or might have missed an opportunity, by staying in school to finish a degree.

Reflecting on my own college experience, I bought into the learning for the sake of learning, liberal arts (un)focus, and I enjoyed it, but I'm not sure it was worth the amount of money my parents spent for a Georgetown degree. Looking back, I had no concept of the cost, and having no plan for post-graduation, I can see why my parents pressured me into going to law school. Because what on earth would I do with an American Studies degree? In my mind, I was leaving my options open, but in reality it was just postponing the time I needed to make a decision.

If I had to do it over again myself, I would take a gap year and try to focus on what I wanted to do for a job after college, so I could study the things that would be useful to me in that job. Yes, I learned to research and write and think and those things serve me well today, but I'm not sure the time and money spent was worth it.

So for my kids, I think it depends.

What kind of preparation did you do before you hit the road?

Though we asked our kids to help with the planning, they were unwilling participants in the beginning. They didn't open the many guidebooks I brought home from the library, and their input consisted solely of telling us they wanted to go to Paris to see the Eiffel Tower and to Tokyo because it sounded cool. My husband and I sketched out a general itinerary, but when we left home, we bought only our first flights to Europe, and planned the first six weeks of our 11-month trip.

In terms of education, we researched various curricula we could use on the road. Some were book-heavy (literally) and would not have been practical since we would be moving so frequently and didn't want to pack an extra suitcase just for books. Some were time-intensive, intending, it seemed, to duplicate the school experience online. That would have taken time away from what we thought would be the most educational aspect of our year: getting out into the world and exploring other cultures.

When researching the requirements for homeschooling in our state, we found two interesting things. First, the requirements for homeschooling were minimal. In Virginia, you only have to show that the children are supervised by someone with a high school degree or more, and you must follow a curriculum, and show evidence of progress at the end of the year. There are no specific curriculum requirements, however, so we submitted a curriculum that we felt confident that we could work with during our travels. We decided to focus on math, world history (instead of the U.S. History they would do at school), reading, writing, art, and Spanish (since we knew we would be in Spanish-speaking countries for four months). We purchased DVD-based math courses for the girls, who are at different levels in math, and a world history textbook.

The second thing we learned, which gave us more confidence in our plan, was that if, at the end of the year, our 'evidence of progress' was not sufficient, the punishment would be a probationary period for the subsequent homeschooling year. Since the girls planned to return to school the next fall, we concluded that no matter what happened, the girls should be able to progress to the next grade level. Still we did do a little celebratory dance when we got the letter saying that the evidence of progress that we submitted was approved.

One of the best parts of roadschooling is being able to use our travels to further the education of our children. Can you give us an example of doing that?

Our daughters were 12 years old when we left the U.S., and would have been heading into 7th grade. Both were strong and enthusiastic readers, so we assigned them some books to read that could tell them a bit about places we were visiting. The Diary of Anne Frank made a good backdrop for our travels through Europe, where evidence of World War II was everywhere. Bill Bryson's Australia was a little dry for their tastes, but we made sure they read the parts about the huge variety of deadly critters Down Under.

We intended to have the girls research and write several paragraphs about each country we visited, but we found that that would have taken too much time. We had them write blog posts for our travel blog, and would edit them.

The world history textbook we brought with us was broken into short chapters covering events around the globe over time, so we sometimes skipped to the sections pertaining to where we stopped. A chapter on the Vietnam War was enlightening to the kids and parents alike as we traveled from South to North in that country.

We made a real effort to use our Spanish skills as we traveled, and we encouraged the girls to ask questions in Spanish whenever we were out. They really built up their confidence in the language quite a bit, especially after we took a one-week Spanish course in Buenos Aires to give them some knowledge of grammar.

We had a good time with our art explorations in museums around the world. Sometimes we would have the girls pick a favorite work in a museum and research and write about it afterwards.

Although school and travel are intricately entwined and we're always working on our children's education, how much time do you spend daily or weekly on 'school stuff?' By that I mean the time spent directly on developing reading, writing, researching, math, or other skills typically taught in school.

It took us a while to settle on a routine. The first few months, the girls would work on their math for an hour or so per day, and we would read and discuss a chapter from their history books each week. They both enjoy reading, so they would read on their own, using their Kindle readers.

There were times when we were traveling that we skipped the planned schooling entirely. We went a month without math work when we were in New Zealand, because we had thought they would be able to work on it while we drove our rented campervan each day, but the roads proved too curvy and nausea-inducing.

Towards the end of the trip, we spent about two hours per day on math, and probably another thirty minutes on writing.

What educational materials do you carry with you?

Each girl carried a netbook, and we had an external DVD player for their DVD-based math courses. The math courses also included a huge 1" thick workbook for each of them. The history book was a little smaller, and we opted for the PDF versions of the activity book and test book for history. Other than that, we did Spanish lessons online, and they read books on their Kindles.

If you could give one piece of advice to a parent considering heading out to travel full time, what would it be?

Trust yourself. And try not to carry too many textbooks.

For more inspiration, visit the Connor family on the web at www.alloverthemap.net.

Lukas and Anders Rasmussen

Meet the Rasmussen brothers – 12-year-old Lukas and 15-year-old Anders. They started their educational journey in public school in the USA, spent some time in international schools, and finally headed into a year of roadschooling while traveling full time.

Tell me about your education. What kinds of things do you do that you consider 'schooling' or 'education.'

Lukas – We went to all sorts of museums and I didn't really feel like anyone was forcing me into doing anything (except maybe once or twice.) That type of attitude helps me learn a lot – more than in regular school. Also, when we were waiting around or just sitting somewhere, we could play games and invent stuff. All of that helps increase our creativity and thinking more. Whenever we are talking, that's a form of education.

Anders – I think education is a much broader term than schooling. I would say every day I had education in some form or another. It was almost all the time informal education, though. Schooling, I think of as doing structured work for the purpose of education, like a traditional school. I didn't do much of this because we were busy with other stuff. But I did do a year of math, which I considered schooling.

What are your goals for your education? Do you hope to go to university? In a perfect world, what would these years of your childhood prepare you for?

Lukas – They would give me a more open mind so that I don't have to be all 'stuck up' and spoiled if I don't like something. I could bear more. If I go to college, even if I don't get what I want, I can still be happy because of roadschooling.

Anders – In my education, I want to learn a lot and have fun too. I want to go to university and I really enjoy learning. In a perfect world, education would completely prepare you for adult life. Roadschooling gives you a great idea of the real world and gives you real experience.

When most people think of school, they think of the 3 R's – Reading, wRiting, and 'Rithmetic. Do you consider that you are below average, average, or above average in those three areas? In other words, do you think you know about as much as kids in traditional educational settings in the basic 3 R's?

Lukas – For our roadschooling, we did have an online math book. We did problems from that. I was two grades up, so I probably know more 'Rithmetic than other people my age. For reading, sometimes we were waiting in places and when we weren't talking, I was reading something. That helped me improve my vocabulary. I am above average in that, too. And wRiting, well, I've been pretty good since before our time on the road. I got a bit behind while roadschooling, but not that much. I'm still way ahead of my peers from before.

Anders – I think I know a lot more about them than the average kid, especially math. During our roadschooling year, I did not learn as much about those subjects as others would have learned in a traditional school.

In what ways do you think your education differs from those in more traditional environments? In which ways is it better? In which ways is it worse?

Lukas – I don't have much homework when we are roadschooling, but I also do less. So, in effect, I learn less. But every day is a field trip, and we're learning so much more about culture and art than we would at regular school. At regular school there is structure; you always know what's going to happen. It's not so exciting, but sometimes it's good to have structure rather than surprises at every turn.

Anders – My year of roadschooling did not give me nearly as much structured learning as I would have had in a traditional school.

However, I learned a lot of things that are impossible to learn in regular school. Overall, roadschooling definitely improved my education.

Think long term – think of yourself as a young adult entering the work force. How do you think your experiences being roadschooled will set you apart from others?

Lukas – I'll have experience in different countries. I'll have more knowledge about some stuff, but know less about other stuff, having not studied it properly.

Anders – There are not many people who have gone through as many experiences as I have. I have a much more global mindset than other kids.

What advice would you give a parent who is considering traveling and roadschooling her children?

Lukas – It's tiring. If you give up, it would be a bad experience for your child(ren), but if you stick with it and you stay firm, then it will be a good experience.

Anders – Don't completely forego structured education. In this world it is still very important to have smarts in the 3 R's and roadschooling definitely does not teach these things unless you make a point of teaching those.

Visit www.4explore.blogspot.com for more information.

Brenon Weed

At the young age of nine months, 15-year-old Brenon Weed took his first cross country trip via train with his parents, a precursor to his future nomadic life. When he was one, his father got a job that required full-time travel, so his parents bought an RV and hit the road in 1999. Since then, he has criss-crossed the country at least a dozen times visiting 45 states, Mexico and Greece. He's earned over fifty Junior Ranger badges with his favorite park being Everglades National Park.

Many of Brenon's favorite learning opportunities happened through volunteer work: he released baby sea turtles in Florida, helped keep an historic train car ferry in Michigan shipshape, delivered meals to homebound AIDS patients in DC, worked on a homestead shearing sheep in Maryland and educated the public at an ocean science center in California.

Tell me about your education. What kinds of things do you do that you consider 'schooling' or 'education.'

I have a fairly broad view of education. I would consider anything that positively adds to myself as a learning experience. Such as, if I read a fantasy book I might learn a new word or how to spell one, or gain some sort of thought-provoking idea that might inspire me to do something or build something, or be a better person.

What are your goals for your education? Do you hope to go to university? In a perfect world, what would these years of your childhood prepare you for?

My goal for my education is to continue learning my entire life, and to keep learning a positive and fun experience.

I don't have any particular motivation to go to a university. I am not opposed to the idea however and if it feels right when I am old enough I suppose I could go.

I would hope my education would prepare me for life. To be adaptable and able to continue learning new things for whatever field I go into.

When most people think of school, they think of the 3 R's – Reading, wRiting, and 'Rithmetic. Do you consider that you are below average, average, or above average in those three areas? In other

words, do you think you know about as much as kids in traditional educational settings in the basic 3 R's?

I feel that for reading I am most likely above average as public schools seem to make reading uninteresting and move it into the 'chore' category, whereas I have always enjoyed reading.

As for writing I feel I fall somewhere average. My grammar is fine (better than some but not noteworthy) and my spelling might be a little above average.

Arithmetic wise I probably fall slightly below the mark. I have all the basic necessities down such as times tables, long division, and algebra but most teens my age are probably moving on to more advanced math.

In what ways do you think your education differs from those in more traditional environments? In which ways is it better? In which ways is it worse?

It differs most notably, in my opinion, in that I am not forced to learn anything. Everything I do is self-motivated and I decide what to learn and when to learn it. I think this is beneficial, to me at least, because it encourages me to view learning in a fun way rather than as a chore.

Socially my education is very different. One of the questions that I am asked most is, "How do you socialize out of school?" which always seemed silly to me. Children socialized before school, and I feel that the traditional schooling environment encourages poor social behavior. Such as people being 'popular' and only playing with children your own age.

Because I am homeschooled, I spend a lot of my time with my family and my brothers. We all get along very well, and when we do argue it rarely lasts long. Because of constantly being in each others' company we sort things out quickly and get to spend lots of time together which I think is very important.

I do feel, however, that in school it is useful to have someone teaching that knows a lot about a certain subject, and can show you things in person, like how to do something. Especially when you get to higher education and they can explain very complicated things.

Think long term – think of yourself as a young adult entering the workforce. How do you think your experiences being roadschooled will set you apart from others?

I think that roadschooling helps give one a bigger picture view. Traveling and seeing new places and different ways of living really opens up your mind to new ideas. I hope I am more creative, ingenuitive, and adaptable.

What advice would you give a parent who is considering traveling and roadschooling their children?

I would recommend they do it. It would offer their kids an experience that will shape them for the rest of their life. Traveling and seeing new places is a wonderful and beautiful thing that they will never forget. Learning on the road and getting to spend time with their families every day is a gift and I believe it is very beneficial.

Theodora Sutcliffe

Freelance writer Theodora Sutcliffe travelled the world solo
with her son for four years and is now based in Bali, Indonesia,
where she continues to explore Asia, both at ground level and
underwater.

What is your basic educational philosophy? How do you see that kids learn?

Children learn in a range of ways, through play, through structured education, through observation and immersion, through reading and researching, all the way through to engaging with their peers online in forums and social media.

My approach to education is fairly conventional: I studied Latin, Greek and Philosophy at university, so I believe that knowledge, however abstruse, has a value of its own, and critical thinking skills are key. Most of us will never use Pythagoras or pi-r squared, but it's part of the sum of human knowledge a well-rounded person should have.

What do you envision for your children long-term in terms of education? University or no? Why do you think university is or is not important?

I benefited a great deal from university, both in terms of thinking skills and in terms of life skills and friendships and socialization and experience: note that I'm British, so my education was free, and I actually got a grant from the government towards my living costs as well.

It's still the case that many career paths are impossible without a degree, and many others are extremely difficult to embark on without that piece of paper. If Zac decided he had something he wanted to do that precluded university, I'd obviously support him. At the moment, though, he wants to go to a good university and do an academic degree.

University's a fantastic experience, and, whether or not he ultimately uses his qualification, I think it's good for him to have that. University also forms an important part of the ongoing separation of parent and child, a safe space to discover the person you are, and build your own friendships – a way to leave home, in short.

What kind of preparation did you do before you hit the road?

Academically? Not a great deal. We had to write out a list of what he'd learn for the homeschool people, so I took the subjects he'd have covered at primary level and made a list of how he'd check those off on our planned one year of travel. It's actually a great exercise, and I'd recommend people do it: list out the subjects they'd be covering in school, and how you can cover those using what's around you on your travels.

I taught briefly in my early 20s, so I didn't think covering the basics of elementary would be an issue – and nor did I think too hard about education as we were only looking at a year.

One of the best parts of roadschooling is being able to use our travels to further the education of our children. Can you give us an example of doing that?

Too many examples! On Pulau Derawan, Indonesia, we snorkeled with turtles, watched them lay their eggs, and Zac helped out at a turtle sanctuary. So we turned that into an essay on the environmental threats to green sea turtles in Indonesia.

More extremely, Zac did a stint in a Chinese school in Harbin – he was the only non-Chinese child there apart from one Korean – to improve his Chinese. Great social skills, great learning, great for language and incredible for math.

Some really easy examples: currency exchange sums and bargaining in markets. Another example? Exploring the pyramids around Cairo, and the Egyptian Museum in Cairo, reading around gods and goddesses, and doing a piece of writing on the gods of Ancient Egypt. Seeing the retreating glaciers en route to Everest base camp proved useful for more environmental science, and celebrating Easter in the Philippines helped with religious education. Arts? Making pottery in Egypt, making silver jewelry in Bali....

Although school and travel are intricately entwined and we're always working on our children's education, how much time do you spend daily or weekly on 'school stuff?' By that I mean the time spent directly on developing reading, writing, researching, math, or other skills typically taught in school.

We spent very little time – although we did do longer stops where Zac was in school for a month or two. Typically, he'd do a piece of writing work every so often, he'd have regular Skype Chinese lessons with a tutor for an hour or so, and we'd go through spasms of math and science. He did nothing for our last few months of travel, because we'd decided we were stopping so he might as well go feral.

At one point he had a very good Skype tutor for math and science, but he went back to full-time work, and we never found anyone as good again. That said, he's now back in fulltime education at an international school in Bali, and after less than a term he's tracking at age, advanced or exceptional for every subject bar PE, where he's behind.

What educational materials did you carry with you?

Laptops, mainly. Also books, digital and otherwise. We did have a Singapore math book and we do have a Chinese text book. That's not the American Singapore Math, which is ludicrously dumbed down, but what a child his age would be learning in Singapore. Texts can easily be found online, as can resources like the Khan Academy and BBC bitesize.

If you could give one piece of advice to a parent considering heading out to travel full time, what would it be?

Just do it! And if it's only for a year or so, especially at elementary age, follow the advice of Zac's London headteacher: "keep up the math and English." Don't try to replicate the school environment. Do get them involved in their own learning and goal setting.

If you're looking at traveling full-time for many years, or with kids of high school age, you need to do some harder thinking. Don't think you can do all the teaching yourself – if you're not good at English, then your kids won't benefit from your teaching, and if you know no science (like me), you'll be teaching them duff science. Keep reviewing what they should know at their age in the conventional school system, and don't skip over the gaps.

Also, don't help them too much with their studies. Children need to learn to edit their own work and settle to their own work without a parent hanging over them helping them.

Don't neglect PE. We did a lot of physical stuff – diving, skiing, horseriding, hiking – but we didn't do anything with a ball for four years, so all that stuff we take for granted in PE classes (running backwards round the gym) had to be learnt from scratch.

And finally – don't trap them into your own life. Just because you want to be an online entrepreneur, doesn't mean your kids have to, or want to, follow that path. Provide them with the options that mean they can be a doctor, a lawyer, a banker if that's where their personality and career journey leads them – don't close their door to uni just because you personally think that the periodic table is a waste of time.

For more information, visit Theodora on the web at www.escapeartistes.com.

Printed in Great Britain
by Amazon